PRESENTED BY:

The Van Wert High School
Class of 1950

ANGELS AND MIRACLES

Time Inc.
HOME ENTERTAINMENT

AMERICAN BIBLE SOCIETY

PUBLISHER
Richard Fraiman
GENERAL MANAGER
Steven Sandonato
EXECUTIVE DIRECTOR, MARKETING SERVICES
Carol Pittard
DIRECTOR, RETAIL & SPECIAL SALES
Tom Mifsud
DIRECTOR, NEW PRODUCT DEVELOPMENT
Peter Harper
ASSISTANT DIRECTOR, NEWSSTAND MARKETING
Laura Adam
ASSISTANT PUBLISHING DIRECTOR,
BRAND MARKETING
Joy Butts
ASSOCIATE COUNSEL
Helen Wan
BRAND & LICENSING MANAGER
Alexandra Bliss
DESIGN & PREPRESS MANAGER
Anne-Michelle Gallero
BOOK PRODUCTION MANAGER
Susan Chodakiewicz

GENERAL EDITOR
Christopher D. Hudson
SENIOR EDITOR
Kelly Knauer
MANAGING EDITOR
Carol Smith

CONSULTING EDITORS FROM THE AMERICAN
BIBLE SOCIETY'S NIDA INSTITUTE FOR
BIBLICAL SCHOLARSHIP:
Barbara Bernstengel
Robert Hodgson, Ph.D.
Charles Houser
Philip H. Towner, Ph.D.
Eric Yost

WITH SPECIAL THANKS TO THE AMERICAN
BIBLE SOCIETY'S COMMITTEE ON TRANSLATION
AND SCHOLARSHIP

CONTRIBUTING WRITERS
Elizabeth Arlene
Stan Campbell
Laura Coggin
Benjamin D. Irwin
Carol Smith

DESIGN AND PRODUCTION
Symbology Creative
Mark Wainwright

SPECIAL THANKS:
Christine Austin
Glenn Buonocore
Jim Childs
Rose Cirrincione
Jacqueline Fitzgerald
Lauren Hall
Jennifer Jacobs
Suzanne Janso
Brynn Joyce
Mona Li
Robert Marasco
Amy Migliaccio
Brooke Reger
Dave Rozzelle
Ilene Schreider
Adriana Tierno
Alex Voznesenskiy
Sydney Webber

© 2009 Time Inc. Home Entertainment

Time Inc.
1271 Avenue of the Americas
New York, New York 10020

ISBN 10: 1-60320-086-X
ISBN 13: 978-1-60320-086-8
Library of Congress Number: 2009928251

We welcome your comments and suggestions about *Angels and Miracles*. Please write to us at:
Angels and Miracles
Attention: Book Editors
PO Box 11016
Des Moines, IA 50336-1016

If you would like to order any of our hardcover Collector's Edition books, please call us at 1-800-327-6388.
(Monday through Friday, 7:00 a.m.–8:00 p.m. or Saturday, 7:00 a.m.– 6:00 p.m. Central Time).

TABLE OF CONTENTS

INTRODUCTION TO ANGELS AND MIRACLES

WHY MIRACLES?

An entire world spoken into existence,
A sea parted, leaving a path of dry land in its wake,
The dead brought back to life,
The sick restored to health . . .

These kinds of extraordinary events appear throughout the Bible. For those who witnessed them, these events, often referred to as miracles, were signs that pointed to a larger meaning. When Moses, for example, stumbled across something like a bush that burned but was not consumed, it not only got his attention—it gave credence to the message he received at the site.

Likewise, for Jews living in the first century, Jesus' miracles drew attention to his ministry and revealed an authority and power the likes of which they had never seen before. The miracles of Jesus demonstrated God's love for the people (Luke 4:18-21) and announced the presence of the Kingdom of God.

In the ancient world, the extraordinary acts we refer to as miracles today were often unexplainable by the expectations, common at the time, of how nature works. Because of their extraordinary nature, these miracles got people's attention, motivating them to consider their source. The events themselves did not create faith, but often were performed for those who already had faith, giving evidence of the hand of God at work on behalf of humanity.

As we read about these miracles today, they invite us, as well, to consider a power beyond ourselves.

A Reading from Deuteronomy 4:35-36

The LORD wants you to know he is the only true God, and he wants you to obey him. That's why he let you see his mighty miracles and his fierce fire on earth, and why you heard his voice from that fire and from the sky.

photo above:
John Everett Millais
Moses at the top of Mt. Horeb holding up his arms during the battle, assisted by Aaron and Hur

READ IT FOR YOURSELF

DEUTERONOMY 29:2–6

Moses called the nation of Israel together and told them:
When you were in Egypt, you saw the LORD perform great miracles that caused trouble for the king, his officials, and everyone else in the country. He has even told you, "For 40 years I, the LORD, led you through the desert, but your clothes and your sandals didn't wear out, and I gave you special food. I did these things so you would realize that I am your God." But the LORD must give you a change of heart before you truly understand what you have seen and heard.

EXODUS 34:10

The LORD said:
I promise to perform miracles for you that have never been seen anywhere on earth. Neighboring nations will stand in fear and know that I was the one who did these marvelous things.

1 CHRONICLES 16:11–12

Trust the LORD
and his mighty power.
Worship him always.
Remember his miracles
and all his wonders
and his fair decisions.

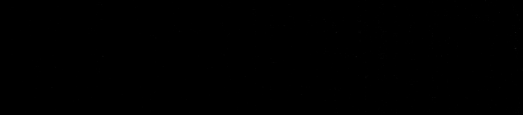

JOB 37:4–7

"God's majestic voice thunders his commands, creating miracles too marvelous for us to understand. Snow and heavy rainstorms make us stop and think about God's power."

Jesus worked many other miracles for his disciples, and not all of them are written in this book. But these are written so that you will put your faith in Jesus as the Messiah and the Son of God. If you have faith in him, you will have true life. — John 20:30-31

FASCINATION WITH THE SUPERNATURAL

Why are people fascinated with all things supernatural?

In all likelihood, because when we marvel or experience awe, we are intrigued by the thought of a world beyond the one we can experience.

The thrill we feel at the possibility of the supernatural is somewhat like the thrill a child experiences when listening to a scary story— we feel the suspense of not knowing what will happen next, of considering a world where someone or something is not obliged to obey the laws we are bound to, and of suspecting there might be something beyond what we experience with our five senses.

The Bible is a book that offers questions as well as answers about the supernatural world. While the people who experienced the extraordinary events described throughout this book held a different perspective on them than the perspective of the modern world, their stories still speak to us. In this modern world where we have so many answers at our fingertips, these events remind us of the mystery that is a part of life and faith.

READ IT FOR YOURSELF

MARK 16:20

Then the disciples left and preached everywhere. The LORD was with them, and the miracles they worked proved that their message was true.

ACTS 14:3

Paul and Barnabas stayed there for a while, having faith in the LORD and bravely speaking his message. The LORD gave them the power to work miracles and wonders, and he showed that their message about his gift of undeserved grace was true.

A Reading from Mark 9:14-24

When Jesus and his three disciples came back down, they saw a large crowd around the other disciples. The teachers of the Law of Moses were arguing with them. The crowd was really surprised to see Jesus, and everyone hurried over to greet him. Jesus asked, "What are you arguing about?" Someone from the crowd answered, "Teacher, I brought my son to you. A demon keeps him from talking. Whenever the demon attacks my son, it throws him to the ground and makes him foam at the mouth and grit his teeth in pain. Then he becomes stiff. I asked your disciples to force out the demon, but they couldn't do it." Jesus said, "You people don't have any faith! How much longer must I be with you? Why do I have to put up with you? Bring the boy to me." They brought the boy, and as soon as the demon saw Jesus, it made the boy shake all over. He fell down and began rolling on the ground and foaming at the mouth. Jesus asked the boy's father, "How long has he been like this?" The man answered, "Ever since he was a child. The demon has often tried to kill him by throwing him into a fire or into water. Please have pity and help us if you can!" Jesus replied, "Why do you say 'if you can'? Anything is possible for someone who has faith!" At once the boy's father shouted, "I do have faith! Please help me to have even more."

photo above:
Meister des Hitda-Evangeliars
Evangeliar der Äbtissin Hitda von Meschede, Szene: Jesus und die Schwiegermutter Petri

The Crossing of the Red Sea
Marc Chagall

MIRACLES

The word miracle usually brings to mind that which is thought impossible—that which defies the laws of nature. But the reason for a miracle is just as important as its occurrence.

Many Old Testament miracles were understood to be signs of God's judgment—a catastrophic flood, the destruction of wicked cities, or the plagues of Egypt, as examples. Others were viewed as God's protection—the sun stopped in its tracks to help an army win a battle or to strike an enemy army blind.

There were also miracles of deliverance and salvation. After leaving Egypt, the Israelites crossed the dry bed of a parted sea; they ate a steady diet of miraculously supplied quail and manna in the desert; and they experienced a deliverance from venomous snake bites. There were also great escapes, like Daniel's deliverance from the lion's den and the protection of his companions in the fiery furnace.

The New Testament records many healing miracles, both during and after the ministry of Jesus. Those who were paralyzed walked again. The dead came back to life. Jesus also performed miracles to provide for people's most basic needs—multiplying food and calming storms.

Perhaps no account engenders more debate than the creation narrative of Genesis 1 (one of several creation narratives in the Bible).

Some view the account as an either/or kind of proposition—a scientific process or a God-induced process. For those ancients who first heard and interacted with this account, however, no such schism existed.

However the modern world chooses to define the process used, according to Genesis, God spoke the world into existence. The first chapter of the Bible describes a six-day structure with God resting from his creative work on the seventh day.

A Reading from Genesis 1:1-2:2

In the beginning God created the heavens and the earth . . .
God said,"I command light to shine!" And light started shining. God . . .
named the light "Day" and the darkness "Night" . . .
—that was the first day.

God said,"I command a dome to separate the water above it from the water below it."
And that's what happened. God . . . named it "Sky" . . .
—that was the second day.

God said,"I command the water under the sky to come together in one place,
so there will be dry ground". . . "I command the earth to produce all kinds of plants,
including fruit trees and grain." And that's what happened . . .
—that was the third day.

God said,"I command lights to appear in the sky and to separate day
from night and to show the time for seasons, special days, and years . . ."
God made two powerful lights, the brighter one to rule the day and the other
to rule the night. He also made the stars . . .
—that was the fourth day.

God said,"I command the ocean to be full of living creatures, and I command
birds to fly above the earth." So God made the giant sea monsters and all the
living creatures that swim in the ocean. He also made every kind of bird . . .
—that was the fifth day.

God said,"I command the earth to give life to all kinds of tame animals,
wild animals, and reptiles". . . God said,"Now we will make humans, and they will
be like us. We will let them rule the fish, the birds, and all other living creatures". . .
God looked at what he had done.

All of it was very good. . . .
—that was the sixth day.

So the heavens and the earth and everything else were created.

By the seventh day God had finished his work, and so he rested.

Creation Described from a Different Point of View

The Bible teaches that God created the world by his wisdom. Proverbs 8 is written from the first-person perspective of Wisdom personified as a woman. In this account, Wisdom describes the world before it took the form that we recognize—oceans, springs, clouds, fields, dust—and describes her own role in the process.

PROVERBS 8:22–31

From the beginning, I was with the Lord. I was there before he began to create the earth. At the very first, the Lord gave life to me. When I was born, there were no oceans or springs of water. My birth was before mountains were formed or hills were put in place. It happened long before God had made the earth or any of its fields or even the dust. I was there when the Lord put the heavens in place and stretched the sky over the surface of the sea. I was with him when he placed the clouds in the sky and created the springs that fill the ocean. I was there when he set boundaries for the sea to make it obey him, and when he laid foundations to support the earth. I was right beside the Lord, helping him plan and build. I made him happy each day, and I was happy at his side. I was pleased with his world and pleased with its people.

CREATION

Human blood cells in vein

Miracle in the Mirror
In the Genesis account, God made human beings on the sixth day of creation. Just as nature reveals a variety of designs working together to sustain life, the human body is like a curtain that, when pulled back, reveals one intricate system after another. We need look no further than our own reflection to see the mystery of God's design. A drop of our blood contains about 250 million cells. There are 1,300 nerve endings in just one square inch of our hand. For the duration of our lives, our hearts never rest for more than a second.

The typical adult human is an example of the miraculous. Made up of 206 bones, covered by twice as many muscles, the body has a system for breathing, blood circulation, digestion, health preservation, and self-healing. We wear our largest organ of all on the outside—our skin. The average adult has at least twenty square feet of it. Our skin is waterproof, self-repairing, and constantly shedding and renewing itself. The human body is yet another miracle in an already marvelous creation.

ABRAHAM & SARAH'S MIRACLE BABY

Abraham and Sarah were quite old when God promised them a miracle: a child of their very own.

And not just any child—their miracle baby would leave a legacy of countless descendants, a whole nation.

Despite the natural odds, God's promise came to pass. At the age of ninety, Sarah gave birth to Isaac.

As difficult as it is for some modern readers to accept that Sarah conceived and bore a child at such an advanced age, it was even more difficult for Abraham and Sarah to believe it. At times they laughed at the idea. On other occasions, they schemed of ways to "help" the promise along.

But it was not Abraham and Sarah's scheming that brought about the miraculous. Nor was it their sometimes faltering faith. Interwoven into this miracle story is the idea that God is always faithful, even when God's people are not.

A Reading from Genesis 18:1-5

One hot summer afternoon while Abraham was sitting by the entrance to his tent near the sacred trees of Mamre, the LORD appeared to him. Abraham looked up and saw three men standing nearby. He quickly ran to meet them, bowed with his face to the ground, and said, "Please come to my home where I can serve you. I'll have some water brought, so you can wash your feet, then you can rest under a tree. Let me get you some food to give you strength before you leave. I would be honored to serve you."

"Thank you very much," they answered. "We accept your offer."

Abraham went quickly to his tent and said to Sarah, "Hurry! Get a large sack of flour and make some bread." After saying this, he rushed off to his herd of cattle and picked out one of the best calves, which his servant quickly prepared. He then served his guests some yogurt and milk together with the meat.

While they were eating, he stood near them under the tree, and they asked, "Where's your wife Sarah?"

"She is right there in the tent," Abraham answered.

One of the guests was the LORD, and he said, "I'll come back about this time next year, and when I do, Sarah will already have a son."

Sarah was behind Abraham, listening at the entrance to the tent. Abraham and Sarah were very old, and Sarah was well past the age for having children. So she laughed and said to herself, "Now that I am worn out and my husband is old, will I really know such happiness?" The LORD asked Abraham, "Why did Sarah laugh? Does she doubt that she can have a child in her old age? I am the LORD! There is nothing too difficult for me. I'll come back next year at the time I promised, and Sarah will already have a son."

Abraham first received the promise of a child directly from God. Later, he played host to guests who confirmed the reality of Sarah's impending pregnancy. According to Genesis 18, three men appeared at the home of Abraham and Sarah. One of those men was identified as "the Lᴏʀᴅ;" the other two were presumed to be angels. It was during this encounter that Sarah overheard the conversation and laughed to herself—only to be heard by their guests and confronted about her faith.

The Bible contains stories of several women who miraculously became pregnant and bore children after years of infertility. In the ancient Near Eastern culture of the Bible, these miracles meant more than just the advent of a child; they represented the preservation of a family name. Childlessness was viewed as a terrible tragedy in the Bible, especially for women. God, however, restored honor to the following women:

REBEKAH After having difficulty conceiving (Genesis 25:21), Rebekah and her husband Isaac (Sarah's son), finally gave birth to twin boys: Jacob and Esau. Jacob became the father of twelve sons and was one of the patriarchs of Israel.

WIFE OF MANOAH AND MOTHER OF SAMSON She was not able to have children, but an angel of the Lᴏʀᴅ appeared to her and told her that she would give birth to a son who would belong to God for as long as he lived (Judges 13).

HANNAH Later in Israel's history, Hannah's years of infertility ended with the promise spoken by a priest named Eli (1 Samuel 1:17). Shortly afterward Hannah conceived and bore a son, Samuel, whose name means "God heard." Samuel became a great prophet of God and anointed the first two kings of Israel.

ELIZABETH In the New Testament, Mary's cousin Elizabeth conceived her son after God spoke to her husband in the temple. The Bible reveals that the birth of their son—who grew up to be John the Baptist—took place when Zechariah and Elizabeth were already quite elderly (Luke 1:7).

The Three Angels Appearing to Abraham, Tiepolo, Giambattista (1696–1770)

THE
BURNING
BUSH

One of the earliest miracles in the Bible involved a bush that caught fire but never burned up.

Perhaps the greater miracle, though, was how God used the burning bush to capture a fugitive's attention and turn him into Israel's great deliverer and lawgiver.

According to the third chapter of Exodus, an "angel of the LORD" appeared to Moses, who had fled to the wilderness after murdering an Egyptian. Throughout the story, God himself is said to speak from the burning bush.

Whether the bush was actually on fire or simply radiated with supernatural presence, it succeeded in its purpose: getting Moses' attention. As Moses approached, God called him by name and introduced himself as the great "I Am." During their conversation, God also announced Moses' mission—to confront the king of Egypt and demand the freedom for the enslaved Israelites.

A Reading from Exodus 3:1-15

One day, Moses was taking care of the sheep and goats of his father-in-law Jethro, the priest of Midian, and Moses decided to lead them across the desert to Sinai, the holy mountain. There an angel of the LORD appeared to him from a burning bush. Moses saw that the bush was on fire, but it was not burning up. "This is strange!" he said to himself. "I'll go over and see why the bush isn't burning up." When the LORD saw Moses coming near, he called him by name from the bush, and Moses answered, "Here I am."

God replied, "Don't come any closer. Take off your sandals—the ground where you are standing is holy. I am the God who was worshiped by your ancestors Abraham, Isaac, and Jacob."

Moses was afraid to look at God, and so he hid his face.

The LORD said:

I have seen how my people are suffering as slaves in Egypt, and I have heard them beg for my help because of the way they are being mistreated. I feel sorry for them, and I have come down to rescue them from the Egyptians.

I will bring my people out of Egypt into a country where there is a lot of good land, rich with milk and honey. I will give them the land where the Canaanites, Hittites, Amorites, Perizzites, Hivites, and Jebusites now live. My people have begged for my help, and I have seen how cruel the Egyptians are to them. Now go to the king! I am sending you to lead my people out of his country.

But Moses said, "Who am I to go to the king and lead your people out of Egypt?"

God replied, "I will be with you. And you will know that I am the one who sent you, when you worship me on this mountain after you have led my people out of Egypt." Moses answered, "I will tell the people of Israel that the God their ancestors worshiped has sent me to them. But what should I say, if they ask me your name?"

God said to Moses:

I am the eternal God. So tell them that the LORD, whose name is "I Am," has sent you. This is my name forever, and it is the name that people must use from now on.

The Bible catalogues numerous appearances of an "angel of the LORD." At times, this mysterious being seemed to be the manifestation of God himself; on other occasions, it seemed to be an angelic being.

While this angel of the LORD sometimes appeared as a mere man who could be touched—and, on one occasion, even wrestled with—sometimes it was simply a voice calling out. The angel of the Lord delivered messages, offered guidance, and on occasion appeared armed with weapons.

Here are some of those who experienced angel sightings in the Bible:

- Hagar, Abraham's servant exiled into the desert (Genesis 16:7–14; 21:17–18)
- Abraham, when he was willing to offer his only son as a sacrifice (Genesis 22:11–12, 15–18)
- Lot, in Sodom, before the city's destruction (Genesis 19:1–22)
- Jacob, after his famous dream of a stairway to heaven (Genesis 28:12; 31:11; 32:1–2)
- Joshua, before the battle of Jericho (Joshua 5:13–15)
- Gideon, while he threshed wheat (Judges 6:11–24)
- Elijah, when an angel served him a meal (1 Kings 19:5–7; 2 Kings 1:3, 15)
- Mary, before becoming pregnant with the Messiah (Luke 1:26–38)
- The women who went to the tomb where Jesus had been buried (Matthew 28:5–7)
- Jesus' disciples, after witnessing Jesus' ascension into heaven (Acts 1:9–11)
- Peter and the apostles, when they were rescued from jail (Acts 5:17–20)
- Peter, when he was rescued from jail (Acts 12:6–10)

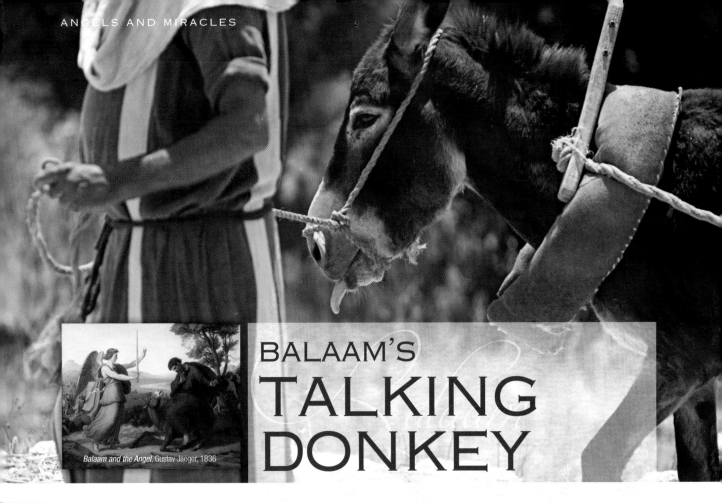

BALAAM'S
TALKING
DONKEY

Balaam and the Angel, Gustav Jaeger, 1836

READ IT FOR YOURSELF

NUMBERS 22:22–35

Balaam was riding his donkey to Moab, and two of his servants were with him. But God was angry that Balaam had gone, so one of the LORD's angels stood in the road to stop him. When Balaam's donkey saw the angel standing there with a sword, it walked off the road and into an open field. Balaam had to beat the donkey to get it back on the road.

Then the angel stood between two vineyards, in a narrow path with a stone wall on each side. When the donkey saw the angel, it walked so close to one of the walls that Balaam's foot scraped against the wall. Balaam beat the donkey again. The angel moved once more and stood in a spot so narrow that there was no room for the donkey to go around. So it just lay down. Balaam lost his temper, then picked up a stick and whacked the donkey. When that happened, the LORD told the donkey to speak, and it asked Balaam, "What have I done that made you beat me three times?"

While many of the Bible's miracles occur in a kind of glorious context, others are set against an unpredictable, even quirky background. Consider the account of the prophet Balaam and—of all things—a talking donkey.

According to the Old Testament book of Numbers, Balaam was hired to pronounce curses on the Israelites as they journeyed to the promised land. On his way to meet the king who had hired him, Balaam's path was blocked three times. Little did Balaam realize that an unseen angel was the source of the obstruction. His donkey, however, was well aware.

First, the donkey dodged the angel by carrying Balaam off the path and into a field. Then he shimmied against a wall, crushing Balaam's foot in the process. Finally, trapped with no way to turn around, the donkey laid down. Balaam responded by beating the animal—at which point, according to the Bible, the donkey spoke. It questioned Balaam for distrusting an animal that had served him so well.

Balaam was suddenly able to see the angel and hear the message he had come to give. Perhaps Balaam's story is a good example of how a miracle can open people's eyes to possibilities they were previously unable to see.

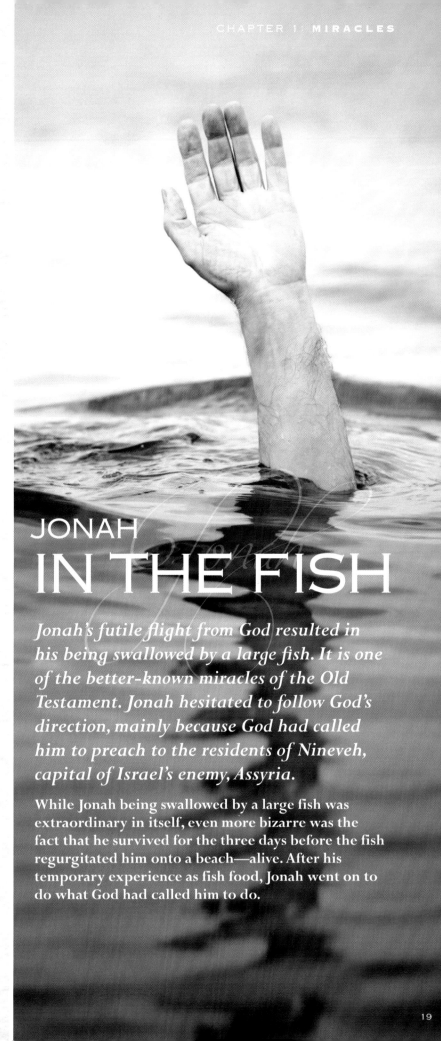

A Reading from
Jonah 1:1-5; 1:12-2:10

One day the LORD told Jonah, the son of Amittai, to go to the great city of Nineveh and say to the people, "The LORD has seen your terrible sins. You are doomed!" Instead, Jonah ran from the LORD. He went to the seaport of Joppa and found a ship that was going to Spain. So he paid his fare, then got on the ship and sailed away to escape.

But the LORD made a strong wind blow, and such a bad storm came up that the ship was about to be broken to pieces. The sailors were frightened, and they all started praying to their gods. They even threw the ship's cargo overboard to make the ship lighter. . . . Jonah told them, "Throw me into the sea, and it will calm down. I'm the cause of this terrible storm."

The sailors tried their best to row to the shore. But they could not do it, and the storm kept getting worse every minute. So they prayed to the LORD, "Please don't let us drown for taking this man's life. Don't hold us guilty for killing an innocent man. All of this happened because you wanted it to." Then they threw Jonah overboard, and the sea calmed down. The sailors were so terrified that they offered a sacrifice to the LORD and made all kinds of promises.

According to the Bible, the LORD sent a big fish to swallow Jonah, and Jonah was inside the fish for three days and three nights.

From inside the fish, Jonah prayed to the LORD his God:

When I was in trouble, LORD, I prayed to you, and you listened to me. From deep in the world of the dead, I begged for your help, and you answered my prayer. You threw me down to the bottom of the sea. The water was churning all around; I was completely covered by your mighty waves. I thought I was swept away from your sight, never again to see your holy temple. I was almost drowned by the swirling waters that surrounded me. Seaweed had wrapped around my head. I had sunk down deep below the mountains beneath the sea. I knew that forever, I would be a prisoner there. But, you, LORD God, rescued me from that pit. When my life was slipping away, I remembered you—and in your holy temple you heard my prayer. All who worship worthless idols turn from the God who offers them mercy. But with shouts of praise, I will offer a sacrifice to you, my LORD. I will keep my promise, because you are the one with power to save. The LORD commanded the fish to vomit up Jonah on the shore. And it did.

JONAH
IN THE FISH

Jonah's futile flight from God resulted in his being swallowed by a large fish. It is one of the better-known miracles of the Old Testament. Jonah hesitated to follow God's direction, mainly because God had called him to preach to the residents of Nineveh, capital of Israel's enemy, Assyria.

While Jonah being swallowed by a large fish was extraordinary in itself, even more bizarre was the fact that he survived for the three days before the fish regurgitated him onto a beach—alive. After his temporary experience as fish food, Jonah went on to do what God had called him to do.

SAMSON'S
SUPERHUMAN
STRENGTH

Samson and Delilah
Anthony van Dyck (1599–1641)

READ IT FOR YOURSELF

JUDGES 16:1–3

One day while Samson was in Gaza, he saw a prostitute and went to her house to spend the night.

The people who lived in Gaza found out he was there, and they decided to kill him at sunrise. So they went to the city gate and waited all night in the guardrooms on each side of the gate.

But Samson got up in the middle of the night and went to the town gate. He pulled the gate doors and doorposts out of the wall and put them on his shoulders. Then he carried them all the way to the top of the hill that overlooks Hebron, where he set the doors down, still closed and locked.

Samson's strength was not of this world. According to the book of Judges, Samson once tore apart a young lion, using only his hands. On another occasion, he killed a thousand Philistines using the jawbone from a donkey's skeleton.

In yet another story, men of a town called Gaza waited to kill Samson as he exited through the city gate. When Samson heard the plot, he left the city in the middle of the night, tearing the gate right out of the ground—doors, posts, bars, and all—and carrying it with him as he departed.

But the most important thing about Samson's story was the source of his power. On the surface, it appeared to be his long hair. In reality, though, Samson's hair was just the sign of a spiritual commitment—his Nazirite vow. This vow meant abstaining from wine and never cutting one's hair, among other things. When Delilah cut Samson's hair, his vow was broken.

In the end, Samson was blinded, enslaved, and forced to work like an animal, turning a millstone to grind grain. Before his life was over, though, he was able to use his miraculous strength—a gift from God—one last time to destroy his captors.

*A Reading from
Judges 14:5-6*

*As Samson and his parents
reached the vineyards near
Timnah, a fierce young lion
suddenly roared and attacked
Samson. But the LORD's Spirit
took control of Samson, and
with his bare hands he tore the
lion apart, as though it had
been a young goat. His parents
didn't know what he had done,
and he didn't tell them.*

Samson Slays the Lion
Francesco Hayez (1791–1882)

2

MIRACLES
OF DESTRUCTION
AND JUDGMENT

Some of the most familiar of the miraculous
events in the Bible were in reality acts of
judgment from God.

The story of Noah's Ark and the animals Noah saved came about
because God saw how evil humans had become, except for Noah.
Only Noah lived right and obeyed God. So God sent a flood that
destroyed all of his creation; only Noah and his family and the
animals on the Ark were saved. God destroyed the cities of Sodom
and Gomorrah because of the wickedness of the people. Other
miracles reveal God as intervening on behalf of people who obeyed
him while issuing a stern judgment on those who did not.
When the Israelites entered the Promised Land, they faced many
battles and confrontations with people who already lived in
the land. The accounts found in the historical books of the
Old Testament describe amazing events, miracles accomplished
not by strength or military prowess, but by the awesome and
unforeseeable actions of God.

photo left:
The Fall of Nineveh
Martin, John (1789–1854)

THE FLOOD

Early on in the book of Genesis, human history is depicted at a low point, when the people God created had become so evil that a catastrophic flood destroyed nearly every living thing on earth. God started over again with a clean slate by means of Noah and his family.

God spared Noah by instructing him to build a boat large enough to house his family and enough animals to repopulate the planet after the flood. Despite the certainty of facing criticism (and even ridicule) from his neighbors, Noah did as God directed.

Once the mighty rain began to fall, it persisted for forty days and nights (Genesis 7:4, 17-18)—God's judgment in tangible form.

Many view the miraculous flood as a demonstration not only of God's justice and judgment but also of God's desire for a new beginning. In the aftermath of the deluge, the rainbow became a symbol to remind every future generation of God's promise that he would never again destroy the earth by flood (Genesis 9:12-17).

READ IT FOR YOURSELF

GENESIS 8:20-22

Noah built an altar where he could offer sacrifices to the LORD. Then he offered on the altar one of each kind of animal and bird that could be used for a sacrifice. The smell of the burning offering pleased the LORD, and he said: Never again will I punish the earth for the sinful things its people do. All of them have evil thoughts from the time they are young, but I will never destroy everything that breathes, as I did this time.

As long as the earth remains,
there will be planting
and harvest,
cold and heat;
winter and summer,
day and night.

A Reading from Genesis 6:5-14, 17-22

The LORD saw how bad the people on earth were and that everything they thought and planned was evil. He was sorry that he had made them, and he said, "I'm going to destroy every person on earth! I'll even wipe out animals, birds, and reptiles. I'm sorry I ever made them."

But the LORD was pleased with Noah, and this is the story about him. Noah was the only person who lived right and obeyed God. He had three sons: Shem, Ham, and Japheth.

God knew that everyone was terribly cruel and violent. So he told Noah:

Cruelty and violence have spread everywhere. Now I'm going to destroy the whole earth and all its people. Get some good lumber a build a boat. Put rooms in it and cover it with tar inside and out. . . . I'm going to send a flood that will destroy everything that breathes! Nothing will be left alive. But I solemnly promise that you, your wife, your sons, and your daughters-in-law will be kept safe in the boat. Take into the boat with you a male and a female of every kind of animal and bird, as well as a male and a female of every reptile. I don't want them to be destroyed. Store up enough food both for yourself and for them.

Noah did everything God told him to do.

Engraving from an antique bible dated 1783

The Dove Sent Forth From the Ark
Gustave Doré

The duration of the rainfall, forty days, is a symbolic span of time associated with several other miraculous events in the Bible.

For example, Moses spent forty days on Mount Sinai at the beginning of the Israelites' journey toward Canaan, which lasted forty years (Exodus 24:18; Numbers 32:13).

Forty days is also the period of time Jesus spent in the wilderness preparing for his ministry—during which time he was tempted by Satan himself (Mark 1:13).

SODOM AND

top left:
The Burning of Sodom
Jean-Baptiste Camille Corot (1796–1875)

right:
Sodom and Gomorrah
John Martin (died 1854)

above:
Salt Pillar in the Dead Sea

To many, the destruction of the cities of Sodom and Gomorrah represents one of the most significant miracles of the Old Testament. The account begins when God informs Abraham that the cities will be destroyed because of the wickedness of their citizens. Abraham, whose nephew Lot lives in Sodom, pleads—even negotiates—for the city to be spared.

Amazingly, God agreed to withhold judgment on Sodom if at least fifty righteous people could be found in the city. Abraham then asked God to spare the city if only forty-five righteous people could be found—then thirty, then twenty. Finally God agreed to save the city if it held only ten righteous people.

Later, when God's messengers arrived in Sodom, Abraham's nephew offered them hospitality, insisting that the visitors stay in his home for the night. But according to Genesis 19, an angry crowd demanded that Lot release his visitors to them. Just as the mob was about to storm the door, the angelic guests miraculously

The sun was coming up as Lot reached the town of Zoar, and the LORD sent burning sulfur down like rain on Sodom and Gomorrah. He destroyed those cities and everyone who lived in them, as well as their land and the trees and grass that grew there.

On the way, Lot's wife looked back and was turned into a block of salt.

Genesis 19:23-26

GOMORRAH

READ IT FOR YOURSELF

GENESIS 18:20–25, 32

The LORD said, "Abraham, I have heard that the people of Sodom and Gomorrah are doing all kinds of evil things. Now I am going down to see for myself if those people really are that bad. If they aren't, I would like to know."

The men turned and started toward Sodom. But the LORD stayed with Abraham. And Abraham asked him, "LORD, when you destroy the evil people, are you also going to destroy those who are good? Wouldn't you spare the city if there are only 50 good people in it? You surely wouldn't let them be killed when you destroy the evil ones. You are the judge of all the earth, and you do what is right." . . .

Finally, Abraham said, "Please don't get angry, LORD, if I speak just once more. Suppose you find only 10 good people there."

"For the sake of ten good people," the LORD told him, "I still won't destroy the city."

intervened, protecting Lot and his household by striking the crowd blind. The men in the bloodthirsty crowd could not even find the doorway to attempt an attack.

At dawn, the angels ordered Lot and his family to flee Sodom without looking back. God was about to destroy the city! Not even ten righteous men were to be found within its gates.

As God's judgment—in the form of burning sulfur—rained down on Sodom and Gomorrah, one person ignored the angels' instructions: Lot's wife. She looked back at the cities as the family fled. Some have suggested that she actually lingered in the city; others say she hesitated and thus was burned in the same way the cities were. The only information provided in Genesis 19 is that she looked back and was instantly turned into a pillar of salt.

The area around the Dead Sea—known for its high salt content—is where many suppose Sodom and Gomorrah were located. Today, at the southern end of that sea, stand several pillars of salt, one of which is famously referred to as Lot's Wife.

GENESIS 19:12–13, 16–17
The two angels said to Lot, "The LORD has heard many terrible things about the people of Sodom, and he has sent us here to destroy the city. Take your family and leave . . .

So the angels took Lot, his wife, and his two daughters by the hand and led them out of the city. When they were outside, one of the angels said, "Run for your lives! Don't even look back. And don't stop in the valley. Run to the hills, where you'll be safe."

THE TEN PLAGUES

The biblical plagues were part of a social and religious confrontation between the God of the Hebrews and the Egyptian Pharaoh, himself regarded as a god by his people.

These ten calamities were brought upon the Egyptians in order to convince the Pharaoh to release his Hebrew slaves, whom he had treated poorly. Moses served as God's liaison to the Egyptian ruler; with each new plague, he warned the Pharaoh of the coming destruction. Speaking for God, Moses demanded that Egypt's king let the Hebrews go free.

The suffering brought about by the first nine plagues was immense, yet it was still not enough to convince the Pharaoh to release the Hebrews. The tenth plague, however, was so devastating that he finally relented. This final plague brought the death of the firstborn son of each family in Egypt. The Israelites were spared when they placed the blood of a sacrificial lamb on the doorposts of their houses—and thus they were "passed over" by the angel of death. This miracle—the plague of death and God's mercy on the Israelites—is remembered in the Jewish feast of the Passover. Christians later connected the sacrificial death of Jesus with the Passover feast, calling Jesus "the Lamb of God" (John 1:29), who shed his blood to offer eternal life to the world.

A Reading from
Exodus 12:23, 29–33

During that night the LORD will go through the country of Egypt and kill the first-born son in every Egyptian family. He will see where you have put the blood, and he will not come into your house. His angel that brings death will pass over and not kill your first-born sons. . . .

At midnight the LORD killed the first-born son of every Egyptian family, from the son of the king to the son of every prisoner in jail. He also killed the first-born male of every animal that belonged to the Egyptians. That night the king, his officials, and everyone else in Egypt got up and started crying bitterly. In every Egyptian home, someone was dead.

During the night the king sent for Moses and Aaron and told them, "Get your people out of my country and leave us alone! Go and worship the LORD, as you have asked. Take your sheep, goats, and cattle, and get out. But ask your God to be kind to me." The Egyptians did everything they could to get the Israelites to leave their country as quickly as possible. They said, "Please hurry and leave. If you don't, we will all be dead."

THE FIRST NINE PLAGUES RECORDED IN EXODUS WERE AS FOLLOWS:

one	The Nile and other water sources in Egypt turned into blood, killing the fish and animals that depended on them (7:14–25).
two	An infestation of frogs descended upon the land (8:1–15).
three	A swarm of lice or gnats tormented the people and their animals (8:16–19).
four	Flies invaded Egypt in such unbearable numbers that people could not go anywhere without encountering them (8:20–32).
five	Disease infected the Egyptians' livestock (9:1–7).
six	Painful boils afflicted the Egyptians themselves (9:8–12).
seven	Hail mixed with fire fell upon the land (9:13–35).
eight	A swarm of locusts appeared, devouring the crops (10:1–20).
nine	A plague of darkness obscured the sun—a devastating assault on Egypt's most revered deity, the sun god Ra (10:21–29).

Elijah and the Priests of Baal
Lucas the Younger Cranach (1515–1586)

READ IT FOR YOURSELF

1 KINGS 18:36-40

When it was time for the evening sacrifice, Elijah prayed: Our LORD, you are the God of Abraham, Isaac, and Israel. Now, prove that you are the God of this nation, and that I, your servant, have done this at your command. Please answer me, so these people will know that you are the LORD God, and that you will turn their hearts back to you. The LORD immediately sent fire, and it burned up the sacrifice, the wood, and the stones. It scorched the ground everywhere around the altar and dried up every drop of water in the ditch. When the crowd saw what had happened, they all bowed down and shouted, "The LORD is God! The LORD is God!"

ELIJAH CHALLENGES
THE 450 PROPHETS OF BAAL

The prophet Elijah was not one to shrink from a fight.

On the heels of a drought—which Elijah believed to be divine judgment brought about because Ahab and Jezebel, Israel's king and queen, promoted the worship of the false god Baal—Elijah made a bold proposition.

Upon seeing the prophet, Ahab denounced him as the "biggest troublemaker in Israel"—hardly indicating a good working relationship between the prophet and the king. Elijah not only returned the insult, calling the king the real troublemaker, but he also berated the people of Israel because they embraced Ahab's false religion. Elijah challenged the Israelites to choose a direction: either worship Baal or worship the God of Israel. To help the people make up their minds, Elijah proposed a test of the powers of the two deities.

With the people of Israel watching in rapt attention, Elijah summoned to Mount Carmel the 450 prophets of Baal and the 400 prophets of the goddess Asherah, another pagan deity. After building two altars—one for Baal's camp and one for the God of Israel—a sacrifice was placed upon both. But no one lit a fire.

Elijah now invited the priests of Baal to implore their gods to send fire to light the sacrifice. Their prayers began in the morning and continued into the evening, to no avail: not even a spark appeared.

Next it was Elijah's turn. Before praying, he ordered the altar of Israel's God to be drenched with water—twelve barrels' worth. A soaked altar would be far more difficult to light, and the land's persistent drought may have lent even greater symbolism to the prophet's surprising command. According to 1 Kings 18, when Elijah asked God to accept his sacrifice, fire suddenly fell from the sky, igniting not only the sacrifice but engulfing the entire altar and scorching the ground all around it.

In the aftermath, the people remembered God's supreme power, the prophets of Baal were slaughtered, and Elijah announced that rain would fall at last over the parched land.

CHARIOT OF FIRE

Elijah's prophetic ministry continued for years following this miraculous event. Though he performed other miracles, perhaps the most remarkable event of his life was its unique ending. While crossing the Jordan River with his apprentice Elisha, Elijah was taken into heaven in a whirlwind by a chariot of fire pulled by flaming horses (2 Kings 2:8).

1

THE WALLS
OF JERICHO

The siege of Jericho was the Israelites' first major victory in what was to become their homeland.

Before crossing the Jordan River to begin the assault, Israel's leader Joshua sent two spies to Jericho for reconnaissance. Trying to elude capture, the spies took refuge in the home of a prostitute named Rahab. In return for protecting them, she asked the spies to spare her family from the coming destruction. Jericho, she revealed, was terrified of Israel's impending assault—even though the city was enclosed within strong walls that served as a powerful fortification.

At the start of the siege, God instructed Joshua that the Israelites should march around the city once a day for six days—not just the military but the entire nation. Joshua obeyed: seven priests armed with trumpets led the procession, followed by the sacred chest known as the Ark of the Covenant, Israel's holiest and most revered possession. On the seventh day, the procession marched around the city seven times, after which the priests blew their trumpets. Only then did the people give the war cry—just as God had instructed. Miraculously, the city's massive walls collapsed at the noise, and the Israelites were able to charge straight into its streets.

The Israelites reduced the city of Jericho into a ruined heap. Only Rahab and her family were spared; her house was the only part of the wall left standing.

A Reading from Joshua 6:12-25

Early the next morning, Joshua and everyone else started marching around Jericho in the same order as the day before. One group of soldiers was in front, followed by the seven priests with trumpets and the priests who carried the chest. The rest of the army came next. The seven priests blew their trumpets while everyone marched slowly around Jericho and back to camp. They did this once a day for six days.

On the seventh day, the army got up at daybreak. They marched slowly around Jericho the same as they had done for the past six days, except on this day they went around seven times. Then the priests blew the trumpets, and Joshua yelled:

Get ready to shout! The LORD will let you capture this town. But you must destroy it and everything in it, to show that it now belongs to the LORD. The woman Rahab helped the spies we sent. So protect her and the others who are inside her house. But kill everyone else in the town. The silver and gold and everything made of bronze and iron belong to the LORD and must be put in his treasury. Be careful to follow these instructions, because if you see something you want and take it, the LORD will destroy Israel. And it will be all your fault.

The priests blew their trumpets again, and the soldiers shouted as loud as they could. The walls of Jericho fell flat. Then the soldiers rushed up the hill, went straight into the town, and captured it. They killed everyone, men and women, young and old, everyone except Rahab and the others in her house. They even killed every cow, sheep, and donkey. The Israelites took the silver and gold and the things made of bronze and iron and put them with the rest of the treasure that was kept at the LORD's house. Finally, they set fire to Jericho and everything in it. (Read the full account in Joshua 5:13–6:27.)

above:
Jericho mudbrick wall

right:
The Taking of Jericho
James Jacques Joseph Tissot (1836–1902)

THE DAY THE SUN

STOOD STILL

The stories of the Israelites' exploits in Canaan reveal many examples of God's faithfulness on their behalf. Perhaps none is as unique as the story of Joshua's battle with the Amorites.

King Adonizedek of Jerusalem, which was not an Israelite city at this time, called on four neighboring cities to fight alongside his army of well-trained warriors. The battle was one of the hardest that Israel faced in its campaign to win the Promised Land.

Joshua and the Israelite army made a surprise attack at night. The Amorite army fled in panic, after an unexpected (and abnormally fierce) hailstorm helped Israel gain the upper hand. The book of Joshua attributes this hailstorm to God's intervention on behalf of the people (Joshua 10:11).

As noon approached, Joshua cried out to God, asking him to do something even more amazing: make the sun and the moon stand still. Even more remarkably, God answered his prayer. The Bible does not indicate exactly how long the sun and moon stood still—a "day" could mean either twelve or twenty-four hours, for instance. In any case, the Israelites defeated their enemies; Joshua's unusual prayer was answered. The miraculous victory was evidence not of his army's prowess but of God's power.

READ IT FOR YOURSELF

JOSHUA 10:9–15

Joshua marched all night from Gilgal to Gibeon and made a surprise attack on the Amorite camp. The LORD made the enemy panic, and the Israelites started killing them right and left. They chased the Amorite troops up the road to Beth-Horon and kept on killing them, until they reached the towns of Azekah and Makkedah. And while these troops were going down through Beth-Horon Pass, the LORD made huge hailstones fall on them all the way to Azekah. More of the enemy soldiers died from the hail than from the Israelite weapons. The LORD was helping the Israelites defeat the Amorites that day. So about noon, Joshua prayed to the LORD loud enough for the Israelites to hear:

"Our LORD, make the sun stop
 in the sky over Gibeon,
 and the moon stand still
over Aijalon Valley."
So the sun and the moon
stopped and stood still
until Israel defeated its enemies.

This poem can be found in The Book of Jashar. The sun stood still and didn't go down for about a whole day. Never before and never since has the LORD done anything like that for someone who prayed. The LORD was really fighting for Israel. After the battle, Joshua and the Israelites went back to their camp at Gilgal.

Joshua Commanding the Sun to Stand Still
Gustave Doré (1832–1883)

THE BLIND ASSYRIAN ARMY

The king of Syria regarded himself as a mighty warrior —yet his best-laid battle plans were constantly thwarted by the Israelites' visionary prophet, Elisha.

Each time the Syrian army set up camp, hoping to catch the Israelite army unaware, Elisha used his prophetic insight to warn Israel's king to steer clear of the area. When the Syrian king discovered who was responsible for ruining his battle plans, he determined to find the culprit and make him answer for his actions.

The king sent his best soldiers to Dothan, Elisha's hometown. When Elisha's servant woke the next morning and realized they were surrounded, he was understandably nervous. But Elisha had confidence that God would protect them. He prayed for his servant to see the reality of the situation, and suddenly the servant was granted a vision: an angelic army—complete with fiery horses and chariots—stood ready to protect the city.

Next, Elisha prayed that God would blind the approaching Syrian army, and once more God obliged. Elisha led the sightless army away from Dothan to the capital city of Samaria, where he prayed that God would restore their sight. Once again, Elisha's prayer was answered.

On Elisha's orders, the Israelites spared the lives of their would-be captives. The Syrians were given a meal and sent on their way. After such a humiliating experience, it was some time before the Syrians staged another attack on the Israelites.

READ IT FOR YOURSELF

2 KINGS 6:13–23

[The Syrians] learned that Elisha was in the town of Dothan and reported it to the king. He ordered his best troops to go there with horses and chariots. They marched out during the night and surrounded the town. When Elisha's servant got up the next morning, he saw that Syrian troops had the town surrounded. "Sir, what are we going to do?" he asked.

"Don't be afraid," Elisha answered. "There are more troops on our side than on theirs." Then he prayed, "LORD, please help him to see." And the LORD let the servant see that the hill was covered with fiery horses and flaming chariots all around Elisha. As the Syrian army came closer, Elisha prayed, "LORD, make those soldiers blind!" And the LORD blinded them with a bright light.

Elisha told the enemy troops, "You've taken the wrong road and are in the wrong town. Follow me. I'll lead you to the man you're looking for." Elisha led them straight to the capital city of Samaria.

When all the soldiers were inside the city, Elisha prayed, "LORD, now let them see again." The LORD let them see that they were standing in the middle of Samaria.

The king of Israel saw them and asked Elisha, "Should I kill them, sir?"

"No!" Elisha answered. "You didn't capture these troops in battle, so you have no right to kill them. Instead, give them something to eat and drink and let them return to their leader."

The king ordered a huge meal to be prepared for Syria's army, and when they finished eating, he let them go.

For a while, the Syrian troops stopped invading Israel's territory.

(Read the full account in 2 Kings 6:8–23.)

Assyrian Fresco

CHAPTER 3

MIRACLES OF DELIVERANCE, SALVATION, AND HEALING

Often the most memorable moments in the
ancient world occurred when God provided for his
people. When God's people were in a pinch,
he often revealed himself as a champion—
leaving the recipients stunned in the midst
of their faith.

So it is with the miraculous events included in this chapter.
On the following pages, you will read about the healing of the sick,
the raising of the dead back to life, the separating of seas into dry
paths, and the transforming of places of destruction and punishment
into abodes of safety. In each of these events, God intervened when
his people needed him most. And today, thousands of years later,
these stories still offer hope to those in need.

WALKING THROUGH WATER

For 430 years the Israelites lived as slaves in Egypt. Everything changed, however, when God called a man named Moses to lead his chosen people to freedom.

Moses petitioned the Egyptian king, or Pharaoh, to let the Israelites leave Egypt. At first, Pharaoh was stubborn and did not want to let the people go. It took ten plagues—including the death of all of Egypt's first-born in a single night—to finally convince Pharaoh to change his mind. The journey from slavery to liberation would prove to be long and arduous, testing the Israelites' faith at every camp and way point.

It did not not take long for Pharaoh to regret his decision to let the Israelites go free—not once he realized that it meant a sizable loss to his labor force. Furious, the king and his forces pursued the Israelites until they finally caught up to them, trapping them against the shores of the Red Sea.

What happened next has become one of the most iconic miracles of the Bible. Moses stretched his walking stick over the sea, and a strong wind blew all night long, dividing the sea until the land was actually dry and the Israelites were able to walk across the seabed (Exodus 14:21-22).

Unfortunately for the Egyptian army, God only kept the sea parted long enough for the Israelites to pass through it. With another stretch of his arm, Moses brought the parted walls of water crashing down on the pursuing Egyptian soldiers, destroying them all. With one last rush of the sea, the Israelites were finally free from more than four centuries of slavery.

A Reading from Exodus 14:15-29

The Lord said to Moses, "Why do you keep calling out to me for help? Tell the Israelites to move forward. Then hold your walking stick over the sea. The water will open up and make a road where they can walk through on dry ground. I will make the Egyptians so stubborn that they will go after you. Then I will be praised because of what happens to the king and his chariots and cavalry. The Egyptians will know for sure that I am the Lord."

All this time God's angel had gone ahead of Israel's army, but now he moved behind them. A large cloud had also gone ahead of them, but now it moved between the Egyptians and the Israelites. The cloud gave light to the Israelites, but made it dark for the Egyptians, and during the night they could not come any closer.

Moses stretched his arm over the sea, and the Lord sent a strong east wind that blew all night until there was dry land where the water had been. The sea opened up, and the Israelites walked through on dry land with a wall of water on each side.

The Egyptian chariots and cavalry went after them. But before daylight the Lord looked down at the Egyptian army from the fiery cloud and made them panic. Their chariot wheels got stuck, and it was hard for them to move. So the Egyptians said to one another, "Let's leave these people alone! The Lord is on their side and is fighting against us." The Lord told Moses, "Stretch your arm toward the sea—the water will cover the Egyptians and their cavalry and chariots." Moses stretched out his arm, and at daybreak the water rushed toward the Egyptians. They tried to run away, but the Lord drowned them in the sea. The water came and covered the chariots, the cavalry, and the whole Egyptian army that had followed the Israelites into the sea. Not one of them was left alive. But the sea had made a wall of water on each side of the Israelites; so they walked through on dry land.

The Red Sea

Crossing of the Red Sea. Miniature from the Codex Landau-Finaly (Visconti-Hours)
Belbello da Pavia (c.1430–1473)

QUAIL AND MANNA

After the triumph of the Exodus, the Israelites' march toward deliverance hit a snag.

Their destination was far away, and in between lay an imposing stretch of desert and mountains. The journey was long and hard, and the Israelites were ill-prepared for it. Quickly they became disillusioned and began complaining—they were hungry, tired of wandering, and undoubtedly felt anxious about the many miles ahead. According to the book of Exodus, their despair festered to the point where they wished they had died in Egypt without God's deliverance. And so they complained to Moses, saying that, when they were Pharaoh's slaves, at least they had food to eat and a place to live!

In the midst of one such moment of disillusionment, God promised to send a special kind of "bread" called manna. Moses, God's representative to the people, instructed each family to gather only as much as they needed for that day. This unusual provision forced the Israelites to trust that God would provide for them day after day. Many Israelites were tempted to hoard the food that covered the ground each day as they awakened, since they didn't know whether more food would come the next day. According to the book of Exodus, some of the people gave in to temptation; but when they tried to keep their surplus food overnight, it would spoil by the following morning, becoming completely inedible.

The daily provision of manna had one more remarkable twist. The people were told to gather twice as much on the sixth day of the week because Moses reported that the LORD had said that the seventh day, the Sabbath, was a sacred day of rest for honoring the LORD (Exodus 16:23-26). As God would later stipulate in the Decalogue, or Ten Commandments, the people were expected to refrain from working on the Sabbath, which was from sundown on Friday to sundown on Saturday. (Exodus 20:8-11). Thus God granted the people a special exception, allowing the people to gather enough manna for two days on the sixth day (Friday). Miraculously, the extra food stayed fresh an extra day.

At first, when God provided manna, he also provided quail. God told Moses that he would provide the Israelites with meat—a nutritious but rare delicacy in an era when most survived on a largely vegetarian diet. Sure enough, quail flew overhead and landed in the Israelite camp.

This happened again later in the journey, and again it followed a bout of complaints from the Israelites. According to Numbers 11:31-34, a strong wind blew the quail into the Israelites' camp, piling the birds three feet high—enough for at least fifty bushels per person. In this case, however, the Israelites paid dearly for their greediness and in not trusting that God would provide for them each day: the LORD afflicted the people with a deadly disease.

A Reading from
Exodus 16:11-18, 31-33

The LORD said to Moses, "I have heard my people complain. Now tell them that each evening they will have meat and each morning they will have more than enough bread. Then they will know that I am the LORD their God."

That evening a lot of quails came and landed everywhere in the camp, and the next morning dew covered the ground. After the dew had gone, the desert was covered with thin flakes that looked like frost. The people had never seen anything like this, and they started asking each other, "What is it?" Moses answered, "This is the bread that the LORD has given you to eat. And he orders you to gather about two quarts for each person in your family—that should be more than enough."

They did as they were told. Some gathered more and some gathered less. Everyone had exactly what they needed, just the right amount. . . .

The Israelites called the bread manna. It was white like coriander seed and delicious as wafers made with honey. Moses told the people that the LORD had said, "Store up two quarts of this manna, because I want future generations to see the food I gave you during the time you were in the desert after I rescued you from Egypt." Then Moses told Aaron, "Put some manna in a jar and store it in the place of worship for future generations to see."

Early Morning in the Wilderness of Shur
Frederick Goodall (1822–1904)

The New Testament writer John referred back to this event. In his Gospel, John recorded a conversation between Jesus and a religious leader named Nicodemus. Jesus compared the saving power of the metal snake to the death that the "Son of Man" (a term Jesus used to refer to himself) would experience in order to provide eternal life to those who believed.

The Brazen Serpent
Anthony van Dyck (1599-1641)

A SNAKE ON A POLE

The Israelites continued to grumble as they wandered in the desert. One of the recurring causes of complaint was their fond memory of life in Egypt (perhaps made vivid by their present circumstances) in contrast to the hardships of the desert.

Eventually, it seems that God grew tired of hearing so many complaints from the Israelites—the people he repeatedly protected. According to Numbers 21:4-9, God sent poisonous snakes into the camp. Only after they bit and killed many Israelites did the people turn to God, admit their error, and ask for help.

In response to Moses' prayer on behalf of the people, God instructed him to make a bronze snake and place it on top of a pole. Anyone who had been bitten could be saved from death by looking at the snake. Moses obeyed God's command, and as a result, those who trusted in God's miraculous mercy lifted their eyes to the bronze snake after being bitten. Thus, their act of faith saved them.

A Reading from Numbers 21:4-9

The Israelites had to go around the territory of Edom, so when they left Mount Hor, they headed south toward the Red Sea. But along the way, the people became so impatient that they complained against God and said to Moses, "Did you bring us out of Egypt, just to let us die in the desert? There's no water out here, and we can't stand this awful food!" Then the LORD sent poisonous snakes that bit and killed many of them.

Some of the people went to Moses and admitted, "It was wrong of us to insult you and the LORD. Now please ask him to make these snakes go away."

Moses prayed, and the LORD answered, "Make a snake out of bronze and place it on top of a pole. Anyone who gets bitten can look at the snake and be saved from death."

Moses obeyed the LORD. And all of those who looked at the bronze snake lived, even though they had been bitten by the poisonous snakes.

The Brazen Serpent
Benjamin West

Elijah

PROPHETS TO THE RESCUE

Besides delivering powerful messages to rulers and the people, Old Testament prophets sometimes performed powerful miracles. The books of 1 and 2 Kings recount miracles performed by two of Israel's great prophets, Elijah and Elisha.

Elijah performed a miracle for a widow struggling to survive during a great drought. The widow had used the last of her flour and oil to make the prophet something to eat. In return, Elijah promised that her provisions would not run out until the drought had ended.

Within a matter of days, the woman's son fell ill and died. Elijah stretched out over the young boy's corpse three times, praying the entire time. Eventually, the boy started breathing again, and Elijah carried him to his grateful mother.

A Reading from 1 Kings 17:8-24

The LORD told Elijah, "Go to the town of Zarephath in Sidon and live there. I've told a widow in that town to give you food."

When Elijah came near the town gate of Zarephath, he saw a widow gathering sticks for a fire. "Would you please bring me a cup of water?" he asked. As she left to get it, he asked, "Would you also please bring me a piece of bread?"

The widow answered, "In the name of the living LORD your God, I swear that I don't have any bread. All I have is a handful of flour and a little olive oil. I'm on my way home now with these few sticks to cook what I have for my son and me. After that, we will starve to death."

Elijah said, "Everything will be fine. Do what you said. Go home and fix something for you and your son. But first, please make a small piece of bread and bring it to me. The LORD God of Israel has promised that your jar of flour won't run out and your bottle of oil won't dry up before he sends rain for the crops."

The widow went home and did exactly what Elijah had told her. She and Elijah and her family had enough food for a long time. The LORD kept the promise that his prophet

Elijah had made, and she did not run out of flour or oil.

Several days later, the son of the woman who owned the house got sick, and he kept getting worse, until finally he died. The woman shouted at Elijah, "What have I done to you? I thought you were God's prophet. Did you come here to cause the death of my son as a reminder that I've sinned against God?"

"Bring me your son," Elijah said. Then he took the boy from her arms and carried him upstairs to the room where he was staying. Elijah laid the boy on his bed and prayed, "LORD God, why did you do such a terrible thing to this woman? She's letting me stay here, and now you've let her son die." Elijah stretched himself out over the boy three times, while praying, "LORD God, bring this boy back to life!"

The LORD answered Elijah's prayer, and the boy started breathing again. Elijah picked him up and carried him downstairs. He gave the boy to his mother and said, "Look, your son is alive."

"You are God's prophet!" the woman replied. "Now I know that you really do speak for the LORD."

The Prophet Elijah
Sassetta (Stefano di Giovanni) (c. 1400–1450)

Elijah was a tough act to follow, but his disciple, Elisha, emulated his mentor. The book of 2 Kings includes two of Elisha's miracles.

Elisha met a woman whose husband had died, leaving her to deal with his debts. She was so deeply in debt that her creditors threatened to enslave her sons. Offering to help, Elisha learned that the woman had nothing to her name but a minimal quantity of oil. Miraculously, the oil multiplied and the woman was able to fill many borrowed jars. With this abundant supply, she was able to sell the oil and pay her creditors, keeping her sons out of slavery.

The same chapter of 2 Kings features a second miraculous event— this one involving a wealthy woman from Shunem, a town frequented by Elisha during his ministry. Over time, Elisha became friends with the woman and her husband, even staying with them whenever he was in town. Grateful for their hospitality, Elisha asked his servant to find out if there was anything he could do for the woman. It seemed that the only thing the woman and her aging husband lacked was a son of their own, so Elisha promised that she would give birth within the year.

Elisha's promise came true, but a few years later, the boy died unexpectedly. Not knowing what to do, the woman threw herself at Elisha's feet and refused to go home without him. Upon arriving at the woman's house, Elisha went to the boy and prayed. Then he stretched himself over the boy's body and—as unusual as it sounds —lay there until his own body heat warmed up the corpse. Miraculously, the boy sneezed seven times and was revived. Elisha then asked his servant Gehazi to summon the boy's mother to pick up her son. (Read the full account in 2 Kings 4:8-37.)

A Reading from 2 Kings 4:1-7

One day the widow of one of the LORD's prophets said to Elisha, "You know that before my husband died, he was a follower of yours and a worshiper of the LORD. But he owed a man some money, and now that man is on his way to take my two sons as his slaves."

"Maybe there's something I can do to help," Elisha said. "What do you have in your house?"

"Sir, I have nothing but a small bottle of olive oil."

Elisha told her, "Ask your neighbors for their empty jars. And after you've borrowed as many as you can, go home and shut the door behind you and your sons. Then begin filling the jars with oil and set each one aside as you fill it." The woman left.

Later, when she and her sons were back inside their house, the two sons brought her the jars, and she began filling them.

At last, she said to one of her sons, "Bring me another jar."

"We don't have any more," he answered, and the oil stopped flowing from the small bottle.

After she told Elisha what had happened, he said, "Sell the oil and use part of the money to pay what you owe the man. You and your sons can live on what is left."

The Prophet Elisha
Sassetta (Stefano di Giovanni) (c.1400–1450)

47

THE FIERY FURNACE

In 605 BC Nebuchadnezzar became king of Babylonia—and a power-hungry king he was. He required his citizens to worship him. He even ordered a ninety-foot-tall statue to be made from gold and put on public display. When the music began to play, everyone was ordered to fall down and worship the statue. Those who didn't were to be thrown into a fiery furnace.

Earlier in Nebuchadnezzar's reign, the Babylonians had sacked Jerusalem and carried many Jews into exile. Among the captives were Shadrach, Meshach, and Abednego, three young men with a strong devotion to God. Because of their faith, they refused to worship any idol made by human hands. Such a blatant violation of the royal decree made Nebuchadnezzar furious; he ordered the furnace to be made seven times hotter than usual before having the three young men tied up and thrown in. According to the Bible, the furnace was so hot that flames leaped out and killed the soldiers who threw the men in.

Yet moments after the men were thrown into the furnace, the king noticed something terrifying—the three were no longer tied up; they were walking around in the furnace! Even more shocking, a mysterious fourth person was walking around with them. When the king had Shadrach, Meshach, and Abednego removed from the furnace, he saw that the fire hadn't harmed them at all. Their hair wasn't burned; their clothes were intact and didn't even smell like smoke.

King Nebuchadnezzar responded by praising Israel's God for sending an angel to protect the men. He applauded their faithfulness and ordered that no people or nation ever speak against their God. The three young Jewish men who defied the king lived to tell about it.

A Reading from Daniel 3:4-29

Then an official stood up and announced:

People of every nation and race, now listen to the king's command! Trumpets, flutes, harps, and all other kinds of musical instruments will soon start playing. When you hear the music, you must bow down and worship the statue that King Nebuchadnezzar has set up. Anyone who refuses will at once be thrown into a flaming furnace.

As soon as the people heard the music, they bowed down and worshiped the gold statue that the king had set up.

Some Babylonians used this as a chance to accuse the Jews to King Nebuchadnezzar. They said, "Your Majesty, we hope you live forever! You commanded everyone to bow down and worship the gold statue when the music played. And you said that anyone who did not bow down and worship it would be thrown into a flaming furnace. Sir, you appointed three men to high positions in Babylon Province, but they have disobeyed you. Those Jews, Shadrach, Meshach, and Abednego, refuse to worship your gods and the statue you have set up."

King Nebuchadnezzar was furious. So he sent for the three young men and said, "I hear that you refuse to worship my gods and the gold statue I have set up. Now I am going to give you one more chance. If you bow down and worship the statue when you hear the music, everything will be all right. But if you don't, you will at once be thrown into a flaming furnace. No god can save you from me."

The three men replied, "Your Majesty, we don't need to defend ourselves. The God we worship can save us from you and your flaming furnace. But even if he doesn't, we still won't worship your gods and the gold statue you have set up."

Nebuchadnezzar's face twisted with anger at the three men. And he ordered the furnace to be heated seven times hotter than usual. Next,

he commanded some of his strongest soldiers to tie up the men and throw them into the flaming furnace. The king wanted it done at that very moment. So the soldiers tied up Shadrach, Meshach, and Abednego and threw them into the flaming furnace with all of their clothes still on, including their turbans. The fire was so hot that flames leaped out and killed the soldiers.

Suddenly the king jumped up and shouted, "Weren't only three men tied up and thrown into the fire?"

"Yes, Your Majesty," the people answered.

"But I see four men walking around in the fire," the king replied. "None of them is tied up or harmed, and the fourth one looks like a god." Nebuchadnezzar went closer to the flaming furnace and said to the three young men, "You servants of the Most High God, come out at once!"

They came out, and the king's high officials, governors, and advisors all crowded around them. The men were not burned, their hair wasn't scorched, and their clothes didn't even smell like smoke. King Nebuchadnezzar said:

Praise their God for sending an angel to rescue his servants! They trusted their God and refused to obey my commands. Yes, they chose to die rather than to worship or serve any god except their own. And I won't allow people of any nation or race to say anything against their God. Anyone who does will be chopped up and their houses will be torn down, because no other god has such great power to save.

above: Detail of the Ishtar Gate

Shadrach, Meshach and Abednego, the Three Youths in the Fiery Furnace of Nebuchadnezzer
Byzantine Mosaic, 11th Century
Location: Monastery Church, Hosios Loukas, Greece

The Bible's accounts of divine miraculous activity continue into the New Testament era with stories of Jesus and his apostles.

Jesus' disciples had witnessed firsthand the miracles of Jesus; and after Pentecost, when they received the Holy Spirit, they, too, began performing amazing acts in the name of their Lord. Acts 3 records one such incident, in which the apostles Peter and John provided an extraordinary display of God's healing power.

In ancient Jerusalem, beggars often sat outside the gates of the Jewish temple. Judaism encouraged almsgiving, the practice of giving money to those in need, so the space around the temple represented prime real estate for those hoping to benefit from the generosity of the devout.

On one occasion, Peter and John were entering the temple when they encountered a man who'd been disabled from birth. Unable to walk, he spent each day begging from the same spot. Peter and John waited for the man to make eye contact with them. When he did, Peter told him they didn't have money—but they did have something to give him. Then Peter told the man to get up and walk in the name of Jesus (Acts 3:6). With that, Peter took the man's hand and helped him to his feet. Though he had never walked before, the formerly disabled man stood up, elated, and jumped his way into the temple!

Because the man had spent so many years outside the temple gate, he was practically a fixture there and was well known to many. Needless to say, the people were awestruck at the sight of him walking. They surrounded Peter and John, curious to know how they were able to make the beggar walk.

READ IT FOR YOURSELF

ACTS 3:2–11

A man who had been born lame was being carried to the temple door. Each day he was placed beside this door, known as the Beautiful Gate. He sat there and begged from the people who were going in.

The man saw Peter and John entering the temple, and he asked them for money. But they looked straight at him and said, "Look up at us!"

The man stared at them and thought he was going to get something. But Peter said, "I don't have any silver or gold! But I will give you what I do have. In the name of Jesus Christ from Nazareth, get up and start walking." Peter then took him by the right hand and helped him up.

At once the man's feet and ankles became strong, and he jumped up and started walking. He went with Peter and John into the temple, walking and jumping and praising God. Everyone saw him walking around and praising God. They knew that he was the beggar who had been lying beside the Beautiful Gate, and they were completely surprised. They could not imagine what had happened to the man.

While the man kept holding on to Peter and John, the whole crowd ran to them in amazement at the place known as Solomon's Porch.

St. Peter
Tempera on wood, Russian Museum, Saint Petersburg

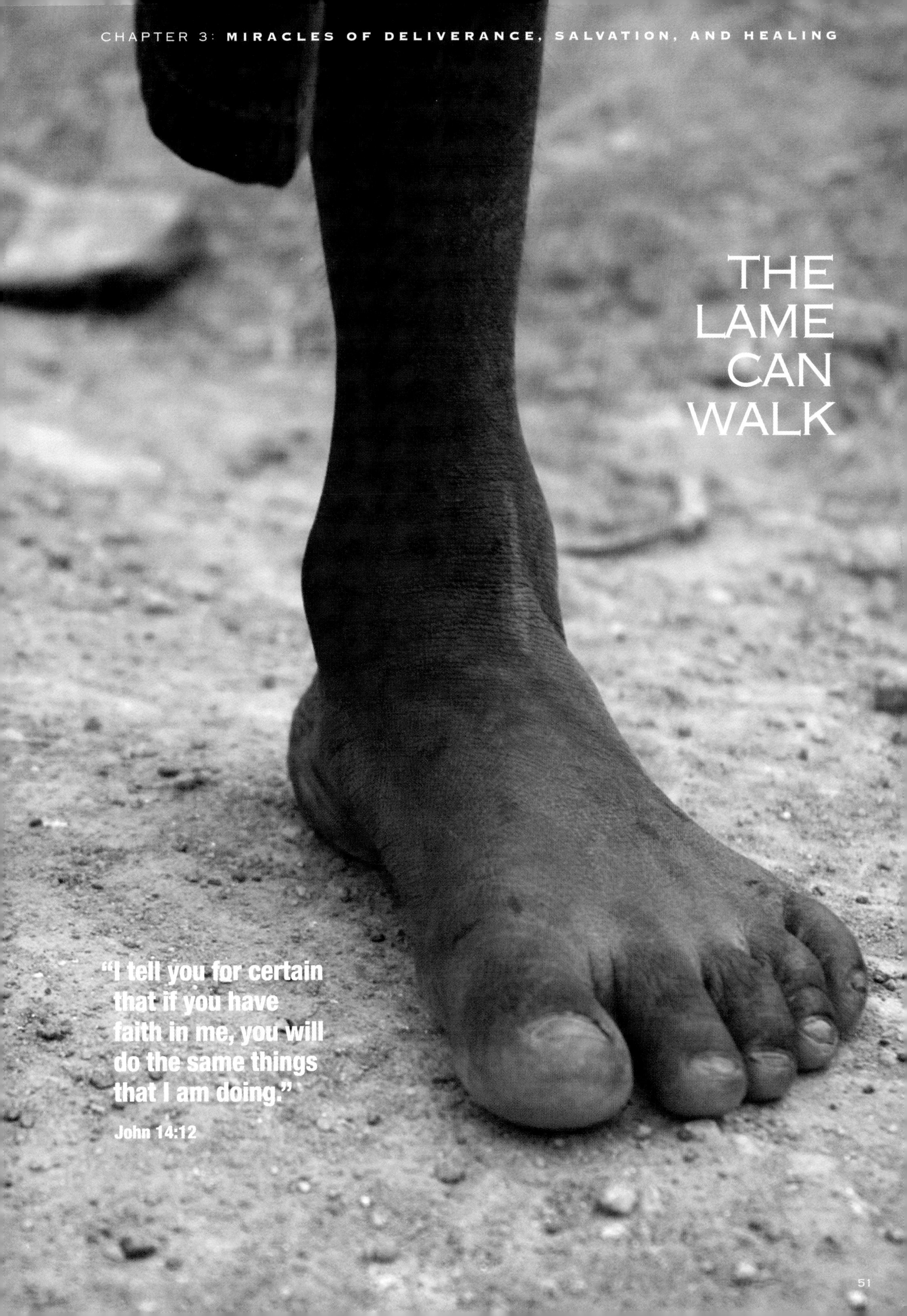

THE
LAME
CAN
WALK

"I tell you for certain
that if you have
faith in me, you will
do the same things
that I am doing."

John 14:12

FIRST-CENTURY PRISON BREAKS

The life of a first-century apostle was anything but boring. The Book of Acts records three different occasions when one or more of the apostles miraculously escaped from prison.

The first account is found in Acts 5:17-25. Much of the apostles' early ministry included healings—a continuation of the work that Jesus had begun to meet people's physical needs. Needless to say, these events attracted large crowds, and the high priest and the Jewish ruling council envied the attention the apostles were receiving. As a result, they had Peter and the others thrown in jail.

This imprisonment didn't last long, however; during the night, an angel freed the apostles. When the high priest sent for them the next day, the jailers found the jail locked and the guards in place, but the cell was empty. The apostles were discovered preaching in the temple.

As the first century progressed, persecution against Christians grew more intense, particularly during the reign of King Herod Agrippa. He had James, one of the disciples who also

READ IT FOR YOURSELF

ACTS 5:17-25

The high priest and all the other Sadducees who were with him became jealous. They arrested the apostles and put them in the city jail. But that night an angel from the Lord opened the doors of the jail and led the apostles out. The angel said, "Go to the temple and tell the people everything about this new life." So they went into the temple before sunrise and started teaching.

The high priest and his men called together their council, which included all of Israel's leaders. Then they ordered the apostles to be brought to them from the jail. The temple police who were sent to the jail did not find the apostles. They returned and said, "We found the jail locked tight and the guards standing at the doors. But when we opened the doors and went in, we didn't find anyone there." The captain of the temple police and the chief priests listened to their report, but they did not know what to think about it.

Just then someone came in and said, "Now those men you put in jail are in the temple, teaching the people!"

happened to be the brother of the apostle John, beheaded. Herod's persecution pleased the Jewish leaders, who saw the early followers of Christ as heretics who had abandoned their Jewish heritage. Eventually, persecution forced these Christians to scatter away from Jerusalem and relocate throughout the region.

During Herod's reign, Peter returned to Jerusalem to meet with the remaining members of the church there. But Herod had Peter thrown in jail and assigned four guards to watch him (Acts 12:1-4). The night before Peter's trial was to begin, an angel appeared in his cell, woke him, and released him from his chains. The angel led Peter out of the cell, past the two pairs of guards, and into the street.

As they were walking away from the jail, the angel disappeared suddenly. At first Peter had thought it was just a dream, but now he was certain that God had sent the angel to rescue him. He made his way to the house of Mary, John's mother, where he shared the story with the believers who had gathered there to pray for his safety.

The third prison-break story is found in Acts 16:16-39. During Paul's second missionary journey, he and his colleague Silas were in Philippi when they met a young girl who was in a double bondage of sorts: she was possessed by a demon and owned as a slave. Her owner made money by having her tell the future, an ability that the author of Acts saw as something made possible by the demonic spirit that controlled her.

The woman followed Paul and Silas for days, yelling about the gospel they were preaching. Exasperated, Paul ordered the demon to leave her body, and it did. This of course infuriated her owners, because not only had the evil spirit departed from her, but the owners could no longer benefit from her sales potential as a seer. In fact, her owners lodged a complaint with the city officials, charging that Paul and Silas were disturbing the peace. As a result, the two missionaries were beaten and thrown in jail, locked in chains, and put under a guard's watch.

At midnight, as the two men prayed and sang while the other prisoners listened, an earthquake shook the jail. The tremor was so violent that the doors burst open, and the chains fell from all the prisoners.

The jailer was, of course, alarmed, thinking the prisoners had all escaped under his watch. Doubtless he would pay with his life for such failure of duty. As the jailer prepared to kill himself rather than face certain execution, Paul stopped him. None of the prisoners had left.

Instead of escaping into the night, Paul and Silas met with the jailer and his family—all of whom came to believe in Paul's message. Paul and Silas returned to the jail that night, but were released the following morning.

READ IT FOR YOURSELF

ACTS 12:6-11

The night before Peter was to be put on trial, he was asleep and bound by two chains. A soldier was guarding him on each side, and two other soldiers were guarding the entrance to the jail. Suddenly an angel from the Lord appeared, and light flashed around in the cell. The angel poked Peter in the side and woke him up. Then he said, "Quick! Get up!"

The chains fell off his hands, and the angel said, "Get dressed and put on your sandals." Peter did what he was told. Then the angel said, "Now put on your coat and follow me." Peter left with the angel, but he thought everything was only a dream. They went past the two groups of soldiers, and when they came to the iron gate to the city, it opened by itself. They went out and were going along the street, when all at once the angel disappeared.

Peter now realized what had happened, and he said, "I am certain that the Lord sent his angel to rescue me from Herod and from everything the Jewish leaders planned to do to me."

ACTS 16:25-31

About midnight Paul and Silas were praying and singing praises to God, while the other prisoners listened. Suddenly a strong earthquake shook the jail to its foundations. The doors opened, and the chains fell from all the prisoners.

When the jailer woke up and saw that the doors were open, he thought that the prisoners had escaped. He pulled out his sword and was about to kill himself. But Paul shouted, "Don't harm yourself! No one has escaped."

The jailer asked for a torch and went into the jail. He was shaking all over as he knelt down in front of Paul and Silas. After he had led them out of the jail, he asked, "What must I do to be saved?"

Both Peter and Paul used their ministries to bring healing to those in need. On more than one occasion, they even took part in raising someone from the dead.

Acts 9 tells of a woman named Dorcas who lived in Joppa. She had a reputation for doing good deeds and giving to the poor. When Dorcas died, her friends sent for Peter, a disciple of Jesus who had a reputation for performing miraculous healings. When Peter saw Dorcas's lifeless body, he prayed. Then he simply commanded her to get up. Just like that, according to the biblical account, she opened her eyes and sat up.

Some time later, as Paul was in the midst of his final missionary journey, he was preparing to say goodbye to the Christian believers in Troas. On his final night there, he gathered a group together and addressed them well into the late hours of the night. While listening to Paul, a young man named Eutychus—who was perched precariously on a window sill—went to sleep and fell out of the window, dropping three floors to the ground.

Eutychus was dead by the time Paul got to him. However, seemingly within minutes, Paul announced to the worried assembly that Eutychus had returned to life.

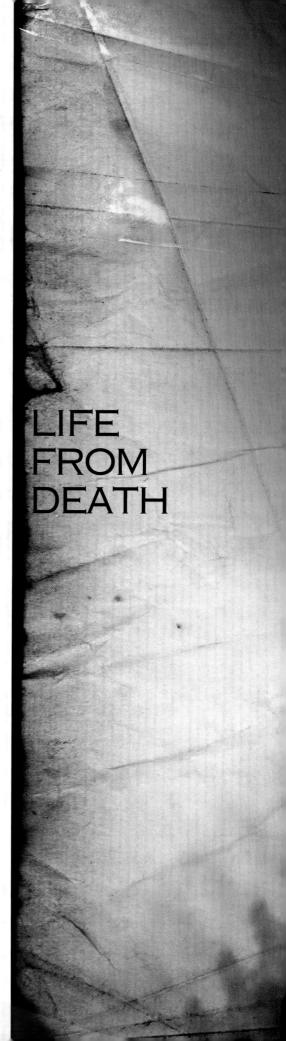

LIFE FROM DEATH

A Reading from Acts 9:36-43

In Joppa there was a follower named Tabitha. Her Greek name was Dorcas, which means "deer." She was always doing good things for people and had given much to the poor. But she got sick and died, and her body was washed and placed in an upstairs room. Joppa wasn't far from Lydda, and the followers heard that Peter was there. They sent two men to say to him, "Please come with us as quickly as you can!" At once, Peter went with them.

The men took Peter upstairs into the room. Many widows were there crying. They showed him the coats and clothes that Dorcas had made while she was still alive.

After Peter had sent everyone out of the room, he knelt down and prayed. Then he turned to the body of Dorcas and said, "Tabitha, get up!" The woman opened her eyes, and when she saw Peter, she sat up. He took her by the hand and helped her to her feet.

Peter called in the widows and the other followers and showed them that Dorcas had been raised from death. Everyone in Joppa heard what had happened, and many of them put their faith in the LORD. Peter stayed on for a while in Joppa in the house of a man named Simon, who made leather.

56   *The Tomb of Lazarus at Jerusalem*
      Anonymous, 19th century

CHAPTER 4

MIRACLES OF JESUS

Jesus' miracles may be the most beloved and best
remembered aspects of his time on earth.
Jesus was a great healer.

Many believe the Old Testament prophet Isaiah foretold the miracles of the
person whom Jews thought would be the Messiah: giving sight to the blind,
enabling the deaf to hear, and making the lame walk. He also healed the
mute, the sick, victims of leprosy, and even brought people back from the
dead. Jesus' followers read these words of Isaiah and reported that Jesus'
miraculous ministry was a testimony to his identity as Messiah and Son of
God. Indeed, some witnesses to Jesus' miracles took the good news to John
the Baptist as the prophet languished in prison—the signs and
wonders performed by Jesus were reassurance that he was, in fact, the
Messiah whom they had been awaiting.

It is important to understand the miracles of Jesus in light of each individual Gospel account. Each of the Gospels was written with a different audience and purpose in mind.

MATTHEW: Matthew wrote to a Jewish audience to represent Jesus as the Messiah foretold in the Old Testament. He includes the miracles of Jesus to help with that representation, and he emphasizes the responses of the people who witnessed the miracles.

MARK: Mark represents Jesus' miracles not as those that lead to faith but that come from faith. Therefore, his account highlights the faith of those interacting with Jesus and receiving blessings from the miracles he performs.

LUKE: Luke's Gospel was written to provide a detailed account of Jesus' life. He emphasizes Jesus' compassion for the sick and the poor, and he connects Jesus' miracles more to the work of the Holy Spirit (*See also* Acts 10:38).

JOHN: John's Gospel was written so that the readers of that Gospel would believe in Jesus and thus receive true life. This Gospel includes seven miracles that function as signs that introduce the teachings of Jesus and emphasize his unique authority.

For the most part, Jesus healed those who demonstrated faith in his power. In several accounts, there seems to be a vital relationship between the miracle performed and the faith of its beneficiary. For example, in the story of the woman who had been bleeding for twelve years (Matthew 9:20; Mark 5:25; Luke 8:43), Jesus declared that it was her faith that healed her. Later, before bringing Lazarus back from the dead, Jesus reminded the crowd that seeing God's glory requires faith (John 11:40).

In one instance, a Gentile (non-Jewish) woman persistently followed Jesus, declaring her faith and asking him to heal her daughter, who was possessed by demons. The disciples were annoyed by the woman's persistence, yet this did not stop her from crying out and begging Jesus to help. Jesus finally answered her: "Dear woman, you really do have a lot of faith, and you will be given what you want." At that moment her daughter was healed. (Matthew 15:28).

As Jesus' reputation for miracles grew, more crowds approached him with their sick and disabled, begging just for a chance to touch his clothes (Matthew 14:34-36; 15:29-31; Mark 6:53-56). And as people witnessed Jesus' miracles or heard of his great works, many put their faith in him.

The author of the Fourth Gospel, whom many identify with the unnamed beloved disciple (John 13:23; 19:26; 21:20), wrote that the miracles of Jesus exceeded the accounts provided in the Gospels. Indeed, the Gospels are not an exhaustive documentation of Jesus' life; instead they introduce us to the service, sacrifice, and compassionate acts of healing that defined the reason for his coming into the world: to seek and save the lost.

The Gospels tell us that those who witnessed Jesus' miracles but lacked faith received harsh words of impending judgment (Matthew 11:20-24; Luke 10:13-16). Jesus' public ministry was defined not only by his healing miracles but also by his teaching and his continual invitation to those who would listen and find spiritual rest in him. While he offered people miraculous healing, for both their physical and spiritual infirmities, Jesus' healing ministry served to announce the Kingdom of God and the restoration of a right relationship with God.

READ IT FOR YOURSELF

ISAIAH 35:5-6

The blind will see,
and the ears of the deaf
will be healed.
Those who were lame
will leap around like deer;
tongues once silent
will shout for joy.
Water will rush
through the desert.

MATTHEW 11:4-6

Jesus answered, "Go and tell John what you have heard and seen. The blind are now able to see, and the lame can walk. People with leprosy are being healed, and the deaf can hear. The dead are raised to life, and the poor are hearing the good news. God will bless everyone who doesn't reject me because of what I do."

JOHN 21:25

Jesus did many other things. If they were all written in books, I don't suppose there would be room enough in the whole world for all the books.

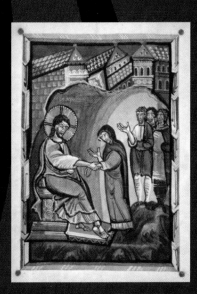

Jesus Healing Peter's Mother-in-Law
c. 1020 Hitda Evangelary, Darmstadt

TURNING WATER INTO WINE

Jesus, who would later become famous for healing the sick and raising the dead, performed his first miracle (as recorded by John) at a wedding feast in the village of Cana, where he turned water into wine in order to save the bridegroom's family from humiliation.

Jesus, along with his mother Mary and his disciples, was a guest at the celebration when the hosts ran out of wine. In a society that valued hospitality so highly, such an embarrassment threatened to tarnish the host family's reputation for years. Mary, who knew better than anyone what her son was capable of, sprang into action. She alerted Jesus to the situation and, despite Jesus' response that his time of public ministry had not yet come, she confidently instructed the servants to do whatever Jesus told them.

Jesus had the servants fill six stone water jars to the top with water. Once they were filled, he instructed them to take a sample to the man hosting the banquet. The host drank the water; only it was not water but wine—and wine of extraordinarily good quality, too. The host called the bridegroom over and expressed his amazement that he had saved the best wine until the end of the feast, when it was customary to serve lower-quality wine. According to John's Gospel, Jesus' miracle at Cana was not only a testimony to his glory and power but also a gift of abundance and celebration.

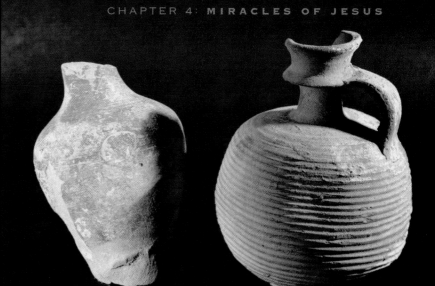

A Reading from John 2:1-11

Three days later Mary, the mother of Jesus, was at a wedding feast in the village of Cana in Galilee. Jesus and his disciples had also been invited and were there.

When the wine was all gone, Mary said to Jesus, "They don't have any more wine."

Jesus replied, "Mother, my time hasn't yet come! You must not tell me what to do." Mary then said to the servants, "Do whatever Jesus tells you to do."

At the feast there were six stone water jars that were used by the people for washing themselves in the way that their religion said they must. Each jar held about 20 or 30 gallons. Jesus told the servants to fill them to the top with water. Then after the jars had been filled, he said, "Now take some water and give it to the man in charge of the feast."

The servants did as Jesus told them, and the man in charge drank some of the water that had now turned into wine. He did not know where the wine had come from, but the servants did. He called the bridegroom over and said, "The best wine is always served first. Then after the guests have had plenty, the other wine is served. But you have kept the best until last!"

This was Jesus' first miracle, and he did it in the village of Cana in Galilee. There Jesus showed his glory, and his disciples put their faith in him.

The gospel writers included their accounts of the miracles of Jesus, not as stand-alone events, but as documentation of Jesus' ministry. In the case of John's Gospel, the miracles recorded often served as signs to everyone around of Jesus' identity. In fact, the word used for miracle in this fourth gospel is a Greek word translated as "sign." The author of this gospel pointed to Jesus as the Son of God and recounted the miracles to confirm that identity.

The Wedding Feast of Cana
[Paulo] Veronese (c. 1528–1588)

A Reading from Luke 8:43-48
(see also *Matthew 9:20-22;*
Mark 5:25-34)

In the crowd was a woman who had been
bleeding for twelve years. She had spent
everything she had on doctors, but none of
them could make her well. As soon as she
came up behind Jesus and barely touched
his clothes, her bleeding stopped.

"Who touched me?" Jesus asked.

While everyone was denying it, Peter said,
"Master, people are crowding all around
and pushing you from every side." But Jesus
answered, "Someone touched me, because I
felt power going out from me." The woman
knew that she could not hide, so she came
trembling and knelt down in front of Jesus.
She told everyone why she had touched him
and that she had been healed at once.

Jesus said to the woman, "You are now well
because of your faith. May God give you
peace!"

HEALING A
CHRONIC
ILLNESS

Sometimes the miraculous healing bestowed by Jesus hinged on the faith of the receiver.

The Gospels according to Matthew, Mark, and Luke tell the story of a woman who had been bleeding for twelve years. According to Old Testament law (Leviticus 15:25-27), such a condition rendered her "ceremonially unclean" and unfit to worship at the temple with her fellow Jews. No one would dare touch her, because doing so would make them unclean as well. The unnamed woman had spent the last of her savings on physicians, but none of them were able to heal her.

Jesus Healing the Hemophiliac Woman
Early Christian Mosaic, Ravenna, Italy

Yet instead of giving in to despair, the woman clung to her faith in Jesus' healing touch. So when she found herself in a crowd of people following Jesus, she seized her opportunity. Reaching out just enough to touch the edge of Jesus' clothing, she was immediately healed. Jesus, who felt the "power going out," asked who had touched him. The woman came forward and told her story. Impressed, Jesus declared that she had been healed because of her faith.

The power of this story is not in the miraculous healing alone, but in the decisive role the woman's faith played in the healing. It was because of her faith that she was healed. There is another lesson in this story: Jesus was not at all concerned at being touched by someone considered unclean; instead he focused on the woman's faith and blessed her with physical and spiritual peace.

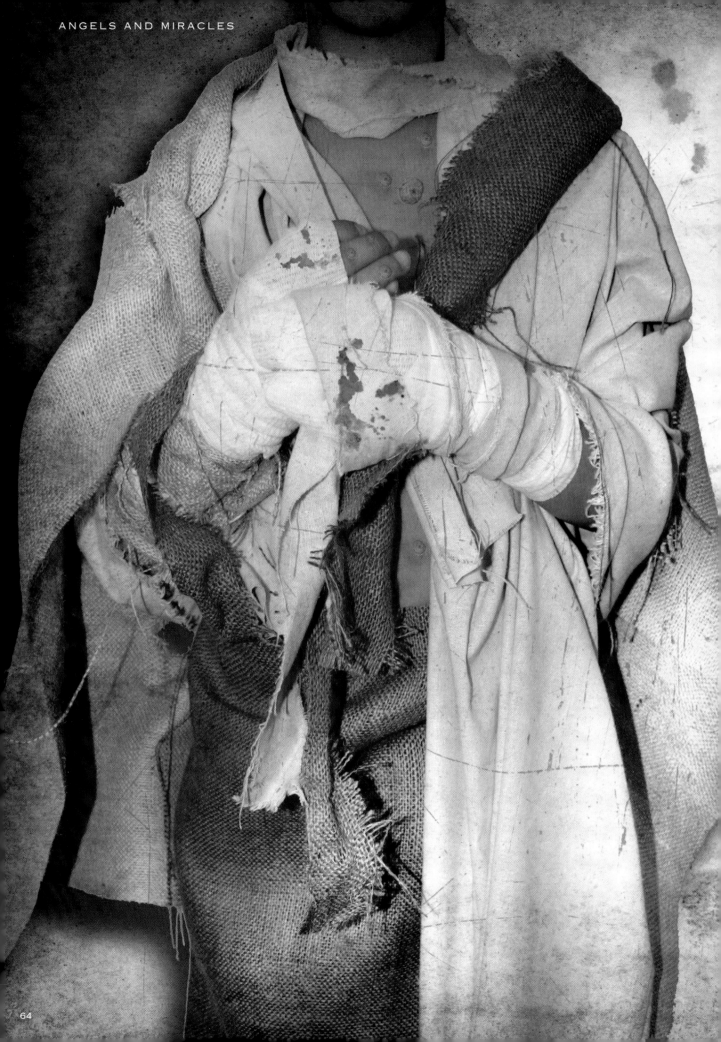

TOUCHING THE UNTOUCHABLE

Imagine being required to live cut off from the rest of society because you were considered untouchable.

That was the fate of victims of leprosy in the ancient world: their disease not only ravaged their bodies; it severed their connection with their community. Lepers were required to tear their clothes, leave their hair uncombed, keep the lower part of their face covered, and go around shouting "I'm unclean! I'm unclean!" (Leviticus 13:45)

Despite his status as a low-class citizen, one leper approached Jesus with a mixture of confidence and humility, kneeling before him and declaring that he believed Jesus had the power to make him well. According to Mark's Gospel, Jesus took pity on the man. What is particularly amazing is that Jesus willingly stretched out his hand and touched the man, despite the contagious nature of leprosy and the reality that by touching the man, Jesus made himself unclean (unfit to worship with other Jews) according to the Law of Moses. In spite of these risks, however, Jesus touched the man, and the man was cured.

Jesus immediately instructed the man to do two things. First, he forbade the man to tell anyone about the miracle. Second, he told the man to present himself to the priest in order to prove that he had been made well. Jesus' second command was in keeping with the Law of Moses regarding the cleansing of lepers (*see* Leviticus 14:2-32). Far from keeping the healing private, this act constituted a very public testimony. This miracle provides yet another example of the connection between a person's faith and Jesus' healing touch.

A Reading from Mark 1:40-45 (see also Matthew 8:1-4; Luke 5:12-16)

A man with leprosy came to Jesus and knelt down. He begged, "You have the power to make me well, if only you wanted to."

Jesus felt sorry for the man. So he put his hand on him and said, "I want to! Now you are well." At once the man's leprosy disappeared, and he was well.

After Jesus strictly warned the man, he sent him on his way. He said, "Don't tell anyone about this. Just go and show the priest that you are well. Then take a gift to the temple as Moses commanded, and everyone will know that you have been healed."

The man talked about it so much and told so many people, that Jesus could no longer go openly into a town. He had to stay away from the towns, but people still came to him from everywhere.

The Parable of Lazarus and Dives
Illuminated manuscript, *Codex Aureus of Echternach*, c. 1035–1040 Germanisches Nationalmuseum, Nürnberg

"Didn't I tell you that if you had faith, you would see the glory of God?"

Rather than rushing to his friend's side, however, Jesus delayed his departure. Eventually, Lazarus died. It was another four days before Jesus could make it to his friend's house in Bethany.

When Jesus arrived at last, some of the mourners wondered aloud why the noted healer—who was known to have given sight to the blind—had not prevented Lazarus's death. Overcome with emotion, Jesus approached the tomb where his friend was buried and made an unusual request: he asked the people to roll away the stone. This was the equivalent of digging up a grave! Martha warned Jesus that there would be an awful smell. After all, her brother had been dead for four days and his body would be decomposing.

Jesus' request was carried out, however.

As soon as the stone was moved aside, Jesus began to pray. He thanked God for always answering his prayers, and then he did something quite perplexing to the onlookers: he called out to the dead man they had buried and for whom they were grieving.

According to John's Gospel, Lazarus responded by walking out of the tomb, still wrapped in his burial cloths. Jesus had given Lazarus new life. In this magnificent miracle, one of the most memorable of Jesus' ministry, we see not only Christ's triumph over the physical state of death, but the promise of a new life for all who heed his call.

A Reading from John 11:33-45 (Read the full account in John 11:1-45.)

When Jesus saw that Mary and the people with her were crying, he was terribly upset and asked, "Where have you put his body?"

They replied, "Lord, come and you will see."

Jesus started crying, and the people said, "See how much he loved Lazarus." Some of them said, "He gives sight to the blind. Why couldn't he have kept Lazarus from dying?"

Jesus was still terribly upset. So he went to the tomb, which was a cave with a stone rolled against the entrance. Then he told the people to roll the stone away. But Martha said, "Lord, you know that Lazarus has been dead four days, and there will be a bad smell."

Jesus replied, "Didn't I tell you that if you had faith, you would see the glory of God?" After the stone had been rolled aside, Jesus looked up toward heaven and prayed, "Father, I thank you for answering my prayer. I know that you always answer my prayers. But I said this, so the people here would believe you sent me."

When Jesus had finished praying, he shouted, "Lazarus, come out!" The man who had been dead came out. His hands and feet were wrapped with strips of burial cloth, and a cloth covered his face.

Jesus then told the people, "Untie him and let him go."

Many of the people who had come to visit Mary saw the things that Jesus did, and they put their faith in him.

Raising of Lazarus
Giotto (1304–1306)

RAISING THE DEAD

Once Jesus was traveling with his disciples when news arrived that Lazarus, the brother of his close friends Mary and Martha, was ill.

*A Reading from John 6:1-14
(see also Matthew 14:13-21;
Matthew 15:32-39;
Mark 6:30-44; Mark 8:1-10;
Luke 9:10-17)*

*Jesus crossed Lake Galilee, which was also
known as Lake Tiberias. A large crowd had
seen him work miracles to heal the sick,
and those people went with him. It was
almost time for the Jewish festival of
Passover, and Jesus went up on a mountain
with his disciples and sat down. When Jesus
saw the large crowd coming toward him,
he asked Philip, "Where will we get enough
food to feed all these people?" He said this
to test Philip, since he already knew what
he was going to do.*

FEEDING THOUSANDS

*Only one of Jesus' miracles is recorded in all four Gospels: the miraculous multiplying of
food for a hungry crowd. In fact, Matthew and Mark tell of two miraculous feeding stories.*

*Philip answered, "Don't you know that it
would take almost a year's wages just to
buy only a little bread for each of these
people?" Andrew, the brother of Simon
Peter, was one of the disciples. He spoke
up and said, "There is a boy here who has
five small loaves of barley bread and two
fish. But what good is that with all these
people?" The ground was covered with grass,
and Jesus told his disciples to tell
everyone to sit down. About
5,000 men were in the
crowd. Jesus took the
bread in his hands and
gave thanks to God. Then
he passed the bread to the
people, and he did the same
with the fish, until everyone had plenty
to eat.*

*The people ate all they wanted, and Jesus
told his disciples to gather up the leftovers,
so that nothing would be wasted. The
disciples gathered them up and filled
twelve large baskets with what was left
over from the five barley loaves.*

*After the people had seen Jesus work this
miracle, they began saying, "This must be
the Prophet who is to come into the world!"*

Each Gospel account paints a slightly different picture of the scene.
John notes that Jesus' disciple Philip protested, arguing that even
many months' wages could not purchase enough food for everyone
present. Matthew, Mark, and Luke reveal to us that the number of
those who ate included about five thousand men. Many scholars
believe the total number of people would likely have far exceeded
this number, since the Gospels, according to the tradition of
the day, did not count the women and children present.

Whatever the precise number, the crowd that gathered
to hear Jesus speak that day was in the thousands, and the
only food they had to start with were five small loaves of bread
and two fish. Jesus spoke a blessing over the miniscule meal and
then, according to all four of the Gospel writers, something amazing
happened: everyone present ate their fill and there were still more
than twelve large baskets of leftovers!

The Church of the Multiplication in Tabgha is the site where
some Christians believe the miracle took place.

This mosaic of the miracle of the loaves and fishes is
located inside the church at Tabgha.

MASTERING THE STORM

Shortly after Jesus multiplied the food, he sent his disciples in a boat onto Lake Galilee, while he stayed behind to pray.

In the middle of the night the winds kicked up and the waters grew choppy. Lake Galilee was known for its unpredictable weather, and now the disciples' boat was being tossed around by the waves. As morning dawned, Jesus approached—walking on the water as if it were dry land! At first his disciples did not recognize him, but he revealed his identity, saying, "Don't worry! I am Jesus. Do not be afraid."

"Don't worry! I am Jesus. Do not be afraid."

As Matthew tells the story, Peter responded, asking Jesus to call him out onto the water. Jesus obliged, and Peter stepped outside of the boat and began to walk across the waves toward Jesus. Quickly reminded of the fierce wind, Peter panicked and began to sink. In his desperation, Peter cried out to Jesus, who reached out and pulled him up. After Jesus brought Peter safely into the boat, the waters calmed.

This was a significant moment for the disciples. Though they had witnessed Jesus perform other amazing feats, this miracle caused them to worship him. While they had already demonstrated their faith in Jesus by following him, this terrifying event prompted them to commit themselves ever more fully to his ministry and his message.

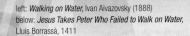

left: *Walking on Water*, Ivan Aivazovsky (1888)
below: *Jesus Takes Peter Who Failed to Walk on Water*, Lluís Borrassà, 1411

A Reading from Matthew 14:22-33
(see also Mark 6:45-52; John 6:16-21)

At once, Jesus made his disciples get into a boat and start back across the lake. But he stayed until he had sent the crowds away. Then he went up on a mountain where he could be alone and pray. Later in the evening, he was still there. By this time the boat was a long way from the shore. It was going against the wind and was being tossed around by the waves. A little while before morning, Jesus came walking on the water toward his disciples. When they saw him, they thought he was a ghost. They were terrified and started screaming.

At once, Jesus said to them, "Don't worry! I am Jesus. Don't be afraid." Peter replied, "Lord, if it is really you, tell me to come to you on the water."

"Come on!" Jesus said. Peter then got out of the boat and started walking on the water toward him.

But when Peter saw how strong the wind was, he was afraid and started sinking. "Save me, Lord!" he shouted.

At once, Jesus reached out his hand. He helped Peter up and said, "You surely don't have much faith. Why do you doubt?"

When Jesus and Peter got into the boat, the wind died down. The men in the boat worshiped Jesus and said, "You really are the Son of God!"

While you can find the same miracle of Jesus listed in more than one Gospel, often the details of the accounts are a little different. This is because each of the Gospels was written with a different purpose and audience in mind.

This account of Jesus walking on water is recorded in three Gospels—Matthew, Mark, and John (Matthew 14:22–33; Mark 6:45–52; John 6:16–21). Matthew and Mark's versions differ only in that Matthew records Simon Peter also walking on the water and Jesus rescuing him. And true to Matthew's mission—to assure his Jewish readers that Jesus was the Messiah—he records the disciples' declaration that they recognized Jesus as the Son of God (Matthew 14:33).

John includes the detail that, after Jesus calmed the waves, the boat suddenly arrived at its destination (John 6:21). Since John wrote to encourage his readers to put their faith in Jesus, including this kind of detail supported his intent.

ILLUMINATING VISION?

The blinding light of the Transfiguration opened the disciples' eyes to Jesus' true identity.

The story is recorded in three of the four Gospels—Matthew, Mark, and Luke. It took place six days after Jesus warned his disciples of his impending suffering and death. Jesus had spoken of the harsh fate that awaited him on three separate occasions, as recorded in Matthew, Mark, and Luke (Matthew 16:21-28; 17:22-23; 20:17-19; Mark 8:31-38; 9:30-32; 10:32-41; Luke 9:22-27; 9:43-45; 18:31-34).

On this occasion, Jesus took Peter, James, and John with him up a mountain. There, he was transformed before their eyes; suddenly his face shone like the sun, and his clothes turned "white as light."

To make the moment even more spectacular, Moses and Elijah, two of Israel's greatest prophets, suddenly appeared and began talking with Jesus.

As the disciples puzzled over this mysterious sight, a cloud descended; from it, the voice of God announced his approval of Jesus. The disciples, terrified at this display of God's presence, fell to the ground. Only after Jesus reassured them, did they return to their feet.

When they opened their eyes, however, the prophets had vanished, and they were again alone with Jesus.

Afterward, Jesus descended from the mountain with his three disciples. He warned them not to tell anyone about what had happened there until after he was raised from the dead.

Years later, the writer of 2 Peter recalled being an eyewitness to the Transfiguration: "When we told you about the power and the return of our Lord Jesus Christ, we were not telling clever stories someone had made up. But with our own eyes we saw his true greatness" (2 Peter 1:16).

top: Mount Tabor in Israel, traditionally identified as the Mount of Transfiguration

bottom: *Transfiguration*
Raphael

A Reading from Matthew 17:1-9 (see also Mark 9:2-13; Luke 9:28-36; 2 Peter 1:16-18)

Six days later Jesus took Peter and the brothers James and John with him. They went up on a very high mountain where they could be alone. There in front of the disciples, Jesus was completely changed. His face was shining like the sun, and his clothes became white as light.

All at once Moses and Elijah were there talking with Jesus. So Peter said to him, "Lord, it is good for us to be here! Let us make three shelters, one for you, one for Moses, and one for Elijah."

While Peter was still speaking, the shadow of a bright cloud passed over them. From the cloud a voice said, "This is my own dear Son, and I am pleased with him. Listen to what he says!" When the disciples heard the voice, they were so afraid that they fell flat on the ground. But Jesus came over and touched them. He said, "Get up and don't be afraid!" When they opened their eyes, they saw only Jesus.

On their way down from the mountain, Jesus warned his disciples not to tell anyone what they had seen until after the Son of Man had been raised from death.

The four gospels included in the New Testament describe the effects of Jesus' Resurrection, for instance the empty tomb and sightings of Jesus. But the *Gospel of Peter*, also an early writing, actually makes an attempt to describe the procession of Jesus out of the tomb. In the description, two men arrive from heaven to assist Jesus out the tomb. As they depart together with Jesus, they are tall enough for their heads to reach the heavens, and the cross follows them. When a voice from heaven calls out, "Thou hast preached to them that sleep," it is the cross that answers in the affirmative.

Many artistic representations of the Resurrection are based on this account.

CONQUERING DEATH

The Resurrection of Jesus is the focal point of the Christian story. Indeed, it is the one miracle on which the entire Gospel message hinges.

The authors of the Gospels all affirm that, three days after his death on the cross, Jesus was raised from the dead.

Matthew wrote that on the Sunday morning after the crucifixion, Mary Magdalene and another woman named Mary had come to anoint Jesus' body, as was the custom of the day. However, before the two women could enter the tomb, an angel appeared and announced that Jesus was no longer dead and no longer present in the tomb.

Luke's Gospel reveals that there were two angels at the tomb on the day of Jesus' resurrection. Similarly, John mentions two angels who spoke to Mary while she was crying. Both writers confirmed that the stone blocking the tomb had been rolled back and that Jesus was no longer inside.

Following his Resurrection, Jesus appeared to his disciples numerous times over the next forty days. In the eyes of the Gospel writers, these appearances served as confirmation of the resurrection miracle. It wasn't simply a few women who had seen Jesus; others interacted with him as well.

According to Luke's Gospel, just hours after Jesus was raised from death, he talked with two of his disciples as they traveled on the road to Emmaus (Luke 24:13-35). That same evening, he appeared to all of his disciples who were gathered in one place (John 20:19). A week later, when Jesus appeared to the disciples a second time, he invited Thomas, who had famously doubted the resurrection of the Messiah, to examine the places where his body had been pierced (John 20:24-29).

Jesus appeared to Paul in dramatic fashion on the road to Damascus, where Paul was blinded by a bright light and then led to faith (Acts 9:1-31). Unlike Jesus' first disciples, Paul had never even met Jesus before this miraculous event, but now he devoted his life to spreading Jesus' message of resurrection and redemption.

A Reading from Matthew 28:1-10 (see also Mark 16:1-8; Luke 24:1-12; John 20:1-10)

The Sabbath was over, and it was almost daybreak on Sunday when Mary Magdalene and the other Mary went to the see the tomb. Suddenly a strong earthquake struck, and the Lord's angel came down from heaven. He rolled away the stone and sat on it. The angel looked as bright as lightning, and his clothes were white as snow. The guards shook from fear and fell down, as though they were dead.

The angel said to the women, "Don't be afraid! I know you are looking for Jesus, who was nailed to a cross. He isn't here! God has raised him to life, just as Jesus said he would. Come, see the place where his body was lying. Now hurry! Tell his disciples he has been raised to life and is on his way to Galilee. Go there, and you will see him. This is what I came to tell you."

The women were frightened and yet very happy, as they hurried from the tomb and ran to tell his disciples. Suddenly Jesus met them and greeted them. They went near him, held on to his feet, and worshiped him. Then Jesus said, "Don't be afraid! Tell my followers to go to Galilee. They will see me there."

Supper at Emmaus, Michelangelo da Caravaggio

left: Tapestry detail from the Vatican museum showing the resurrection of Jesus Christ

Jesus' ascension into heaven took place on the Mount of Olives, a large hill that was about a half mile from Jerusalem and halfway between Jerusalem and Bethany. As the moment of parting drew near, the disciples wondered aloud if God was going to restore Israel's autonomy by giving her a king once more. In response to this, Jesus spoke his final words to the disciples. First, he assured them that they did not need to know the timing of future events that were in God's control. Also, he promised that the Holy Spirit would come, giving them guidance and power. Then he repeated his command for them to spread his message to Jerusalem and beyond.

With that, Jesus was taken into heaven right before their eyes. His followers were so awestruck that, although Jesus was no longer there, they just kept staring at the sky. Suddenly, two men dressed in white clothes appeared and explained that Jesus had been taken to heaven and that he would return someday in the same way he had left.

Jesus' ascent into heaven is considered an event that connects the Jesus of history with the Christ of faith. The apostle Paul and other writers of letters found in the New Testament testify to Christ's ascension and his enthronement at God's right hand (Romans 8:34; Ephesians 1:20-21; Colossians 3:1). The author of the letter to the Hebrews writes, "We have a great high priest, who has gone into heaven, and he is Jesus the Son of God … who sits at the right side of God's great throne in heaven. … He went into heaven and is now there with God to help us." (4:14a; 8:1b; 9:24b)

FROM HERE TO HEAVEN

According to Luke's Gospel (24:44-53) and the Book of Acts (1:1-11), Jesus' return to heaven, also known as his ascension, was one last teachable moment for his disciples.

A Reading from Acts 1:3-11

For 40 days after Jesus had suffered and died, he proved in many ways that he had been raised from death. He appeared to his apostles and spoke to them about God's kingdom. While he was still with them, he said:

"Don't leave Jerusalem yet. Wait here for the Father to give you the Holy Spirit, just as I told you he has promised to do. John baptized with water, but in a few days you will be baptized with the Holy Spirit."

While the apostles were still with Jesus, they asked him, "LORD, are you now going to give Israel its own king again?" Jesus said to them, "You don't need to know the time of those events that only the Father controls. But the Holy Spirit will come upon you and give you power. Then you will tell everyone about me in Jerusalem, in all Judea, in Samaria, and everywhere in the world." After Jesus had said this and while they were watching, he was taken up into a cloud. They could not see him, but as he went up, they kept looking up into the sky.

A small shrine commemorating the Ascension, Jerusalem

Suddenly two men dressed in white clothes were standing there beside them. They said, "Why are you men from Galilee standing here and looking up into the sky? Jesus has been taken to heaven. But he will come back in the same way you have seen him go."

The Ascension, St. Mark Cathedral, Venice

"…He went into heaven and is now there with God to help us."

The Ascension from the Mount of Olive
James Jacques Joseph Tissot (1836–1902)   77

PORTRAITS OF
ANGELS

WHEN READING THROUGH THE BIBLE, YOU'RE BOUND TO COME ACROSS AN ANGEL OR TWO AT SOME POINT. AS DESCRIBED IN SCRIPTURE, ANGELS ARE MESSENGERS AND MEDIATORS, SOMETIMES APPEARING IN HUMAN FORM, SOMETIMES IN SPIRITUAL FORM. SOME, WE ARE TOLD, OBEDIENTLY SERVED GOD, WHILE OTHERS REBELLED, CHOOSING INSTEAD TO WORK IN OPPOSITION TO GOD.

SOME PEOPLE TODAY CLAIM TO HAVE SEEN AN ANGEL AT SOME POINT IN THEIR LIVES, BUT A PERSONAL ENCOUNTER IS NOT NECESSARY IN ORDER TO BELIEVE IN THE EXISTENCE OF THESE CELESTIAL BEINGS. IN FACT, SCRIPTURE SUGGESTS THERE IS A VAST MULTITUDE OF ANGELS. WHILE NO EXACT COUNT IS GIVEN, THE FOLLOWING REFERENCES PAINT AN IMPRESSIVE PICTURE: "THOUSANDS OF HIS WARRIORS" (DEUTERONOMY 33:2); "COUNTLESS THOUSANDS" (DANIEL 7:10); "THOUSANDS OF MIGHTY CHARIOTS" (PSALM 68:17); "MORE THAN TWELVE ARMIES [OR LEGIONS]" (MATTHEW 26:53—ESTIMATED AT ANYWHERE FROM 36,000–72,000); "THOUSANDS AND THOUSANDS" (HEBREWS 12:22); "MILLIONS AND MILLIONS" (REVELATION 5:11).

CELESTIAL SPIRITS

A READING FROM DEUTERONOMY 33:2

The LORD came from Mount Sinai.
From Edom, he gave light
to his people,
and his glory was shining
from Mount Paran.
Thousands of his warriors
were with him, and fire
was at his right hand.

top: Icon showing the three Angels hosted by Abraham,
Andrei Rublev
above: Detail of *Jesus Appearing to the Three Marys*
Laurent de la Hyre

THE BIBLICAL TERM THAT WE TRANSLATE AS ANGEL MEANS "MESSENGER," AN INDICATION OF THE PRIMARY ROLE THESE SPIRITUAL BEINGS PLAY IN SCRIPTURE.

In Hebrew, there is no one term that corresponds to the word angel in English. In the Old Testament portion of the *King James Version* of the Bible, the following words, for example, are used to describe these celestial beings: "saints" (Psalm 89:5, 7), "watchers" (Daniel 4:13, 17, 23). In the New Testament, the Greek term *angelos* is translated as angel, but the following usages referring to angels can also be found: "heavenly host" (Luke 2:13) and "ministering spirits" (Hebrews 1:14).

The Bible offers few clues as to what angels look like. Contrary to popular belief, the image of a slender, winged woman is not supported by Scripture. One thing we do know is that when angels appear to people in the Bible, they tend to look like people. Consider Lot's encounter in Genesis 19:1–2, for example: "That evening, while Lot was sitting near the city gate, the two angels arrived in Sodom. When Lot saw them, he got up, bowed down low, and said, 'Gentlemen, I am your servant.'" Lot showed no indication that he knew the true identity of his guests.

Just Who Are They, Anyway?

Angels are sometimes described as being clothed in white, like the "young man in a white robe" who met some of Jesus' followers inside the empty tomb on Easter Sunday (Mark 16). On other occasions, they radiate with the glory of the Lord, like the angel who announced Jesus' birth to the shepherds (Luke 2:9). Aside from these sparse descriptions, though, we know little else about the appearance of angels—making them all the more mysterious to people today.

Abraham and the Three Angels
James Jacques Joseph Tissot (1836–1902)

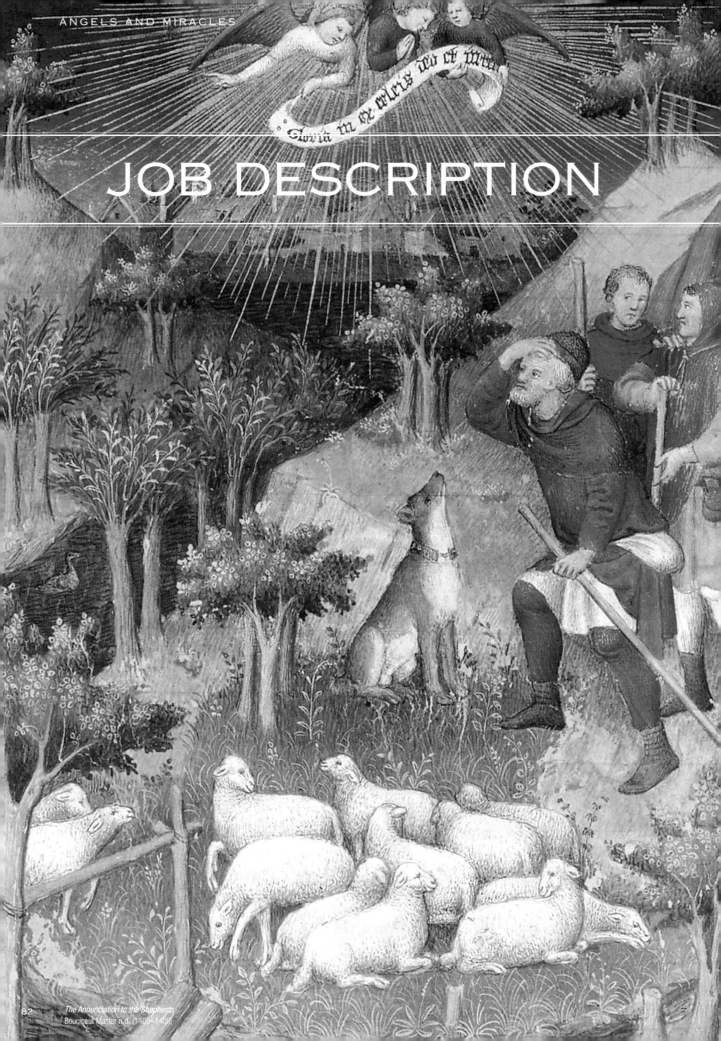

JOB DESCRIPTION

The Annunciation to the Shepherds
Boucicaut Master n.d. (1405–1408)

What Do Angels Do?

THE BIBLE DESCRIBES ANGELS AS BEINGS—SOMETIMES CELESTIAL, SOMETIMES TAKING EARTHLY FORM—WHO EXIST TO DO GOD'S BIDDING—WHATEVER THAT MAY ENTAIL.

Most often, this means serving as a sort of divine messenger. For example, an angel once appeared to a group of shepherds outside Bethlehem, announcing an epoch-shifting event: "I have good news for you, which will make everyone happy. This very day in King David's hometown a Savior was born for you. He is Christ the Lord" (Luke 2:10-11). The birth of Jesus would not be the last momentous event to be heralded by angels. According to Luke 24:6, after Jesus' Resurrection, two angels

delivered news of his Resurrection to the women at the tomb:

"Jesus isn't here! He has been raised from death."

Read the full account of Jesus' Resurrection in Luke 24:1-35.

Sometimes the message the angels delivered was one of encouragement, and sometimes that encouragement took the form of more than just words. Whether it was protecting three young men inside a fiery furnace (Daniel 3), or rescuing the apostles from prison (Acts 5:19), angels occasionally served as God's instruments of protection for his people. According to the writer of Hebrews, angels serve those "who are going to be saved" (1:14).

In the Bible, angels provide not only physical protection and support but spiritual strength and encouragement as well.

Both Matthew and Mark say that angels came to help Jesus when he was in the desert for 40 days (Matthew 4:11; Mark 1:13). Luke's Gospel reports that an angel appeared to Jesus as he prayed for the strength to yield to God's will that he suffer and die (Luke 22:43).

However, angelic labors were not always positive and encouraging. There were times when God's emissaries enacted his judgment on the wickedness of the world. For example,

above: ***Massacre of the Innocents***, Relief from the Pulpit, 1297–1301 Pisano, Giovanni (1248-c.1314)

Genesis 19 describes the fate of the corrupt towns of Sodom and Gomorrah, when two angels appeared at Lot's home in Sodom to warn him of the coming destruction. It was also an angel who struck down King Herod Agrippa for trying to steal honor that belonged only to God (Acts 12:23). And the book of Revelation includes several scenes in which angels serve as instruments of God's judgment on the wicked (Revelation 8:6–9:21 and 16:1-17).

In each of these angelic appearances, the overarching purposes are to mediate the presence and will of God and to glorify and praise God. They are instruments of God's mercy and justice in the world, even when God's judgment is stern.

MISCONCEPTIONS ABOUT ANGELS

detail from:
Spanish Actions Deflected by the Taking of Ghent
Charles Le Brun (1619–1690)

ANGELS WERE NOT CREATED BY GOD

Perhaps this idea came from the fact that angels were not mentioned in the biblical accounts of creation (Genesis 1–2). In the New Testament, however, the Bible clearly confirms that angels were created by God: Paul writes about this in Colossians 1:15-16:

"Christ is exactly like God, who cannot be seen. He is the first-born Son, superior to all creation. Everything was created by him, everything in heaven and on earth, everything seen and unseen, including all forces and powers, and all rulers and authorities. All things were created by God's Son, and everything was made for him."

ANGELS ARE MATERIAL BEINGS

As noted earlier, the Bible records a number of episodes in which angels appear in human form, but these instances are temporary manifestations of a spiritual being in physical form. In Genesis 32, for example, Jacob wrestled an angel; the patriarch's hip was dislocated in the process. And in Genesis 18, three men appear to Abraham and Sarah to announce that a son will be born to them. Elsewhere, the biblical authors seem to understand angels as immaterial creatures without physical bodies. The writer of Hebrews calls them "spirits" (1:14). Paul refers to fallen angels as "rulers of darkness and powers in the spiritual world" (Ephesians 6:12). Both Gospel writers, Matthew and Luke (the author of Acts), identify demons (another name for fallen angels) as "evil spirits" (Matthew 8:16; Acts 19:12). The apparent lack of a material body is a key element that sets these celestial beings apart from humans.

BECAUSE THE BIBLE PROVIDES RELATIVELY FEW DETAILS ABOUT THE NATURE OF CELESTIAL BEINGS, A NUMBER OF TRADITIONS REGARDING ANGELS HAVE DEVELOPED THAT ARE NOT ACTUALLY SUPPORTED BY SCRIPTURE.

Some common misunderstandings explained

ANGELS ARE DIVINE

The longest passage about angels (Hebrews 1–2) describes them as superior to humans but inferior to Christ. The author of Hebrews states that God's Son was also a messenger (1:2), but because of the special Father/Son relationship between Jesus and God (1:5), Jesus is superior to any angel. Therefore, angels are commanded by God to worship God's Son (1:6). In the biblical narrative, angels act strictly as God's servants, carrying out his plans and delivering messages on God's behalf. Angels do have free will, and those in heaven choose to obey God (Matthew 6:10), while those who chose to rebel have been cast into a dark pit until the day of judgment (2 Peter 2:4; Jude 6), when they will be sent into an everlasting fire (Matthew 25:41). God alone is infinite and has the power to create and destroy.

Given that angels are not infinite, it is little surprise to learn that they are not all-knowing, all-powerful, or present everywhere. The Bible reserves such characteristics for God alone. While angels seem to have access to knowledge surpassing our own (see, for example, Galatians 3:19), their knowledge does have limits (Matthew 24:36; Luke 12:8). Angels are subject to the power of God, and they exist to fulfill God's plans (Psalm 103:20).

Last, it is worth noting that Satan was a fallen angel (Luke 10:18), according to many traditions, and even his power is limited—as can be seen in his confrontation with God in the book of Job or his ultimate fate as described in Revelation.

ANGELS ARE DEAD OR GLORIFIED HUMANS

Perhaps one of the most popular ideas about angels is that they are dead humans who have been glorified by God in some special way. Some people take comfort in the belief that their deceased relatives watch over them from heaven. However, the Bible does not equate angels with humans who have died. As noted previously, angels do not seem to be material beings with physical bodies.

But in the future world no one who is worthy to rise from death will either marry or die. They will be like the angels and will be God's children, because they have been raised to life.

LUKE 20:35–36

FALLEN ANGELS

A READING FROM LUKE 10:17–20

When the 72 followers returned, they were excited and said, "Lord, even the demons obeyed when we spoke in your name!" Jesus told them:

"I saw Satan fall from heaven like a flash of lightning. I have given you the power to trample on snakes and scorpions and to defeat the power of your enemy Satan. Nothing can harm you. But don't be happy because evil spirits obey you. Be happy that your names are written in heaven!"

URIEL: FIRE OF GOD

2 Esdras, also called Apocalypse of Esdras, is included in the Apocrypha, a group of early Jewish writings that is sometimes included with the Protestant Bible. The book is made up of seven visions, the first of which includes an angel named Uriel. As Esdras laments his people's affliction, Uriel informs him that the past is longer than the future will be. The rest of the visions regard the end of the age.

Uriel, whose name means "Light or Fire of God," also appears in the Book of 1 Enoch (also from the Apocrypha). In this book, Uriel teaches Enoch the secrets of the sun and is identified as the angel that spoke of the coming deluge (1 Enoch 72–83).

Though a lesser-known angel than Gabriel or Michael, Uriel also appears in Milton's *Paradise Lost* and Haydn's oratorio, *The Creation*.

IF WE THINK WE KNOW LITTLE ABOUT GOD'S ANGELS AND THEIR WORK IN THE WORLD, WE KNOW EVEN LESS ABOUT THEIR FALLEN COUNTERPARTS.

Typically included in this category are demons and the apparent head of all demonic powers, Satan (also known as the devil). But how did fallen angels become fallen, and what is their work in the world? These are questions on which Scripture is fairly silent. But the biblical narrative seems to offer a few tantalizing clues.

Many biblical scholars agree that fallen angels were originally good, like everything else God created. However, they rebelled against God and became evil and were cast out of heaven (away from God's presence), resulting in their "fallen" state. This understanding is based primarily on two New Testament passages that refer to angels who left their "proper places" and "sinned" (2 Peter 2:4; Jude 6). The author of 2 Peter went on to compare the state of the fallen angels to the state of wicked humans who will eventually be subject to judgment (see John 12:31).

Satan, who is sometimes seen as the head of the fallen angels, seems to be a demon himself (see Matthew 12:24, 27 and Luke 10:17-20). In the Hebrew language of the Old Testament, the name Satan is a form of a verb that means "to act as an adversary." Several other terms used for Satan reveal specific aspects of his character: adversary, tempter, enemy, evil one, father of lies, great dragon, and deceiver, to name a few. For examples of his deceptive nature, see such passages as Genesis 3, 2 Corinthians 11:14-15, 1 Thessalonians 2:18, and Revelation 12:9, along with the Gospel accounts of the temptation of Jesus (Matthew 4:1-11; Mark 1:12-13; Luke 4:1-13), the parable of the weeds (Matthew 13:24-30, 36-43), or Judas's betrayal of Jesus (John 13:21-30).

For their part, the demons seem to follow Satan's lead, occupying themselves with tempting and deceiving people—all in an effort to keep them alienated from God. In some passages of Scripture, the "mischief" seems to include causing both mental and physical torment (*see* Matthew 12:22; Mark 9:17; Acts 8:7; Ephesians 6:12).

As intimidating a prospect as demonic possession may be, the Bible declares that all is not lost against Satan and the demons. Throughout the Bible, God's power trumps the power of evil. The book of Job, for example, hints at the limited nature of Satan's power, in contrast to God's. The author of the letter of James promises believers that if they resist the devil, "he will run from you" (4:7). We can also take heart that Scripture predicts a final outcome in which good wins and evil is destroyed forever.

SPIRITUAL WARFARE

Him the Almighty Power Hurled Headlong Flaming From the Eternal Sky
Gustave Doré

THE IDEA THAT THERE IS SOME KIND OF INVISIBLE, SPIRITUAL WAR GOING ON AROUND US CAN BE DIFFICULT TO GRASP. NEVERTHELESS, THE BIBLE HINTS THAT SUCH A CONFLICT BEGAN WITH THE FALL OF THE ANGELS (LUKE 10:18). ALTHOUGH VICTORY WAS MADE CERTAIN BY CHRIST'S RESURRECTION, ULTIMATE SUCCESS WILL NOT BE ACHIEVED UNTIL EVIL IS PUNISHED ONCE AND FOR ALL AT THE END OF TIME.

The Battle of Good and Evil

An example of spiritual warfare can be seen in the temptation of Jesus (Matthew 4:1-11). According to Matthew, Mark, and Luke, Satan tried to entice Jesus to test God. The tempter even quoted Scripture in an effort to convince Jesus to worship him instead of God, but Jesus refused. After Satan left, angels appeared to assist Jesus, who had been weakened by his forty-day fast in the desert. Many see the battle in the wilderness as a foreshadowing of Jesus' road to the cross, where he would be tempted by Satan once more to abandon the work God had sent him to do (Hebrews 2:14-15).

There were also a number of incidents when Jesus encountered people who were regarded as demon-possessed. The interactions between Jesus and the demons provide further insight into the spiritual conflict. According to Luke's Gospel, when Jesus encountered a man possessed by several demons, they begged Jesus not to torture them. So instead, Jesus cast them into a herd of pigs nearby

(Luke 8:26-36). This is just one of many instances in the New Testament in which Jesus publicly confronted and defeated demons who were wreaking havoc in people's lives.

The visions captured in the book of Revelation describe a final, cataclysmic battle between good and evil, resulting in the final defeat of all that is evil. Revelation 12 describes war

from heaven to the earth. In anger, the dragon wages war against those who are faithful to God (Revelation 17).

At the end of this battle, however, the great deceiver—"the devil who fooled them"—is thrown permanently into a burning lake (Revelation 20:10).

A READING FROM MATTHEW 4:1-11

The Holy Spirit led Jesus into the desert, so that the devil could test him. After Jesus had gone without eating for 40 days and nights, he was very hungry. Then the devil came to him and said, "If you are God's Son, tell these stones to turn into bread." Jesus answered, "The Scriptures say:
'No one can live only on food. People need every word that God has spoken.'"
Next, the devil took Jesus into the holy city to the highest part of the temple. The devil said, "If you are God's Son, jump off. The Scriptures say: 'God will give his angels orders about you. They will catch you in their arms, and you won't hurt your feet on the stones.'"
Jesus answered, "The Scriptures also say, 'Don't try to test the Lord your God!'"
Finally, the devil took Jesus up on a very high mountain and showed him all the kingdoms on earth and their power. The devil said to him, "I will give all this to you, if you will bow down and worship me."
Jesus answered, "Go away Satan! The Scriptures say: 'Worship the Lord your God and serve only him.'" Then the devil left Jesus, and angels came to help him.

breaking out in heaven; the Archangel Michael and his mighty army of angels take arms against a dragon and those loyal to it (Revelation 12:7). The enemies of God are thrown

Christ Glorified in the Court of Heaven
Fra Angelico (Guido di Pietro) (c.1387–1455)

ANGELS
BY NAME

THEIR APPEARANCES IN THE BIBLE ARE FLEETING AND OFTEN SHROUDED IN MYSTERY. THEY HAVE THE ABILITY TO INSPIRE AWE AND TERROR, HOPE AND FEAR. YET WITHIN THE PROTESTANT CANON WE MEET ONLY A HANDFUL OF INDIVIDUAL ANGELS—AND ONLY TWO (NOT COUNTING THE FALLEN ANGEL SATAN) ARE INTRODUCED BY NAME: GABRIEL AND MICHAEL. STILL, THESE POWERFUL SPIRITUAL BEINGS OFTEN PLAY AN IMPORTANT ROLE IN THE BIBLICAL STORY.

Michael is identified by the New Testament as an "archangel," a term meaning "chief angel." Whether or not he is the only archangel remains unclear, but he is the only one so named in the Bible.

Gabriel appears four times in the Bible—each time delivering a vital message. Some speculate that Gabriel is also an archangel because he, like Michael, is identified by name. However, this assumption goes beyond what little the Bible reveals about Gabriel.

Even those angels whose names remain a secret are beings of awesome power, capable of instilling a sense of foreboding. For example, the Bible mentions a destroying angel—or the angel of death—who carries out God's judgment on the world.

Angels are merely spirits sent to serve people who are going to be saved.

— Hebrews 1:14

Seraphim make just two appearances in the Bible, but each time it is clear that they play an important role in God's order. The term is derived from the Hebrew word seraph, which, when used as a verb, means "to burn." When used as a noun, it means "a fiery, flying serpent." This somewhat terrifying image seems to suggest a kind of angelic creature that takes the form of a winged serpent such as the flaming creatures that appeared in Isaiah's vision (Isaiah 6:2).

The cherubim are sometimes understood to be a relatively lower class of beings. Some versions of the Bible (including the CEV) refer to cherubim as "winged creatures," perhaps because that is the physical characteristic most often associated with this type of angelic being. One description of cherubim can be found in Exodus 25:18-20; images of these winged creatures were fashioned out of gold and adorned the Sacred Chest (Ark of the Covenant).

Icon of the Archangel Michael
Egyptian School (18th century)

AS "ONE OF THE STRONGEST GUARDIAN ANGELS" (DANIEL 10:13), THE ARCHANGEL MICHAEL SEEMS TO BE ALWAYS READY FOR A FIGHT. HE IS FIRST MENTIONED IN DANIEL 10, WHEN ANOTHER SPIRITUAL BEING APPEARS TO DANIEL IN ANSWER TO THE AGING PROPHET'S PRAYER. THIS IMPOSING CREATURE EXPLAINED THAT HE WOULD HAVE ARRIVED SOONER, BUT THE PRINCE (OR "GUARDIAN ANGEL") OF PERSIA HAD DETAINED HIM. ONLY WHEN MICHAEL CAME TO HIS RESCUE WAS THE NAMELESS CREATURE ABLE TO COMPLETE HIS MISSION AND DELIVER HIS MESSAGE TO DANIEL.

MICHAEL

The Archangel Michael
Guido Reni

This bizarre story may suggest that one of the archangel's duties is to protect and take command over the other angels. To some, the reference to "one of the strongest guardian angels" indicates that there is more than just one archangel.

In addition to his dual roles as protector of the angels and guardian of Israel, Michael directly confronts Satan in two scenes of the Bible. In one encounter, the two argue over the body of Moses (see Jude 9). Despite his power, Michael refuses to insult the devil, instead leaving all judgment of him to God.

A READING FROM REVELATION 12:7-9

A war broke out in heaven. Michael and his angels were fighting against the dragon and its angels. But the dragon lost the battle. It and its angels were forced out of their places in heaven and were thrown down to the earth. Yes, that old snake and his angels were thrown out of heaven! That snake, who fools everyone on earth, is known as the devil and Satan.

The next book, Revelation, describes a great war pitting Michael and his angels against Satan and the fallen angels who are loyal to him. Michael and his angelic warriors gain the upper hand, driving Satan out of heaven and down to the earth, where he wreaks havoc.

The term archangel, meaning "chief or first angel," is used only two times in the Bible (1 Thessalonians 4:16; Jude 9). The name Michael means "Who is like God?"

Daniel 10 also identifies Michael as "the guardian angel of Israel" (10:21). This idea is repeated in Daniel 12:1 "Michael, the chief of the angels, is the protector of your people, and he will come at a time of terrible suffering, the worst in all of history."

READ IT FOR YOURSELF

JUDE 9

Even Michael, the chief angel, didn't dare to insult the devil, when the two of them were arguing about the body of Moses. All Michael said was, "The Lord will punish you!"

IF MICHAEL IS AN ICONIC HEAVENLY WARRIOR, THEN GABRIEL SEEMS TO BE AN ULTIMATE HEAVENLY MESSENGER. TWICE GABRIEL APPEARS IN THE OLD TESTAMENT BOOK OF DANIEL; ON ONE OCCASION THIS ANGEL IS DESCRIBED AS FLYING IN VERY SUDDENLY (DANIEL 9:21). WHETHER THIS IS A LITERAL DEPICTION OR SIMPLY THE AUTHOR'S WAY OF SAYING THAT GABRIEL APPEARED SUDDENLY IS UNKNOWN, BUT IT IS THE CLOSEST THING TO A DESCRIPTION OF GABRIEL TO BE FOUND IN THE BIBLE.

GABRIEL

Each time Gabriel appeared to Daniel, this angelic messenger interpreted a dream that Daniel didn't understand. The first time, Gabriel caused such alarm that Daniel fell trembling to the ground (Daniel 8:17). On the second occasion, Daniel seemed to recognize the heavenly creature and wasn't as afraid (Daniel 9:20-27).

Following the story of Daniel, Gabriel disappears from the biblical record until the New Testament, when the angel delivers perhaps the most important news of all: the coming of the Messiah. First, Gabriel appeared to the priest Zechariah (Luke 1:8-20), who reacted precisely the same way that Daniel had: with fear. Gabriel comforted Zechariah and promised him a son. This son would grow up to be John the Baptist, the first-century prophet who announced the ministry of Jesus, his cousin.

In a final appearance in the Bible, Gabriel announced to Mary that she would give birth to a son: the Messiah who would be named Jesus (Luke 1:26-38).

The name Gabriel means "God is my warrior"

The Angel Who Heals
A lesser-known angel, Raphael, is an angel who heals a man's blindness. He is mentioned in the book called Tobit, part of the Old Testament in Roman Catholic and Orthodox Bibles. Raphael's name means "God heals." The Catholic Church commemorates Raphael along with Michael and Gabriel in the month of September.

A READING FROM LUKE 1:26-38

One month later God sent the angel Gabriel to the town of Nazareth in Galilee with a message for a virgin named Mary. She was engaged to Joseph from the family of King David. The angel greeted Mary and said, "You are truly blessed! The Lord is with you."

Mary was confused by the angel's words and wondered what they meant. Then the angel told Mary, "Don't be afraid! God is pleased with you, and you will have a son. His name will be Jesus. He will be great and will be called the Son of God Most High. The Lord God will make him king, as his ancestor David was. He will rule the people of Israel forever, and his kingdom will never end."

Mary asked the angel, "How can this happen? I am not even married!"

The angel answered, "The Holy Spirit will come down to you, and God's power will come over you. So your child will be called the holy Son of God. Your relative Elizabeth is also going to have a son, even though she is old. No one thought she could ever have a baby, but in three months she will have a son. Nothing is impossible for God!"

Mary said, "I am the Lord's servant! Let it happen as you have said." And the angel left her.

Gabriel, Laura James (1991)

THE DESTROYING ANGEL

THE ANGEL OF DEATH

THE TERM "DESTROYING ANGEL"—ALTERNATIVELY KNOWN AS "THE
ANGEL THAT BRINGS DEATH" (EXODUS 12:23)—LEAVES LITTLE TO THE
IMAGINATION. THE NAME SAYS IT ALL. BEYOND THAT, WHAT IS KNOWN
ABOUT THE DESTROYING ANGEL CENTERS ON THREE PASSAGES OF
SCRIPTURE. NOWHERE IS THE DESTROYING ANGEL NAMED. WE DO NOT
EVEN KNOW WHETHER THE THREE PASSAGES REFER TO THE SAME
ANGEL OR SIMPLY DESCRIBE A TASK THAT ANY ANGEL CAN PERFORM.
IN FACT, PSALM 78:49 ALLUDES TO "SWARMS OF DESTROYING ANGELS."

The first mention of a destroying angel is in Exodus 12. The great leader Moses is in the midst of his legendary confrontation with Pharaoh, trying to persuade the stubborn ruler to release the Israelites from slavery in Egypt. Nine devastating plagues had failed to soften Pharaoh's heart, but for the final plague, God sent the "angel that brings death" to kill the firstborn son of every Egyptian family (12:23). This same angel spared—or passed over—the firstborn sons of the Israelite families.

The next time a destroying angel appears in Scripture is during the reign of King David (2 Samuel 24:1-17). In his pride, David took a census to count how many fighting men were in his army. As punishment for David's conceit, God sent a destroying angel to afflict the nation with a debilitating disease —perhaps meant to serve as a painful reminder of the nation's fragility. Soon, however, God took pity on the people and stopped the mission.

The third appearance of a destroying angel is in 2 Kings 19. At the time, Hezekiah was king of Judah, and the capital city of Jerusalem was under siege by King Sennacherib and the Assyrian army. When Hezekiah cried out for deliverance, God sent a destroying angel to the Assyrian camp, and the angel killed 185,000 men (2 Kings 19:35).

A destroying angel brought death; but more importantly, its appearance served as a sobering reminder that God is sovereign over the events of the world.

The Firstborn Slain, Gustave Doré

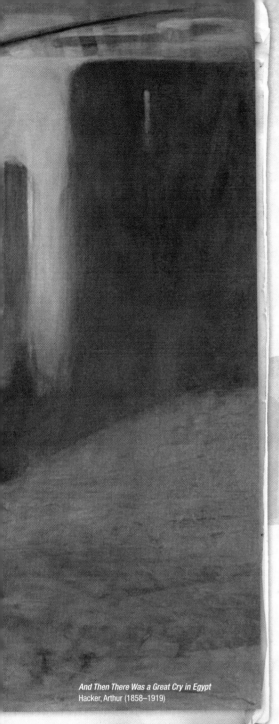

And Then There Was a Great Cry in Egypt
Hacker, Arthur (1858–1919)

READ IT FOR YOURSELF

HEBREWS 11:27-28

Because of his faith, Moses left Egypt. Moses had seen the invisible God and wasn't afraid of the king's anger. His faith also made him celebrate Passover. He sprinkled the blood of animals on the doorposts, so that the first-born sons of the people of Israel would not be killed by the destroying angel.

A READING FROM EXODUS 12:29-31

At midnight the LORD killed the first-born son of every Egyptian family, from the son of the king to the son of every prisoner in jail. He also killed the first-born male of every animal that belonged to the Egyptians. That night the king, his officials, and everyone else in Egypt got up and started crying bitterly. In every Egyptian home, someone was dead.

During the night the king sent for Moses and Aaron and told them, "Get your people out of my country and leave us alone! Go and worship the LORD, as you have asked."

THE CHERUBIM OF THE BIBLE BEAR LITTLE RESEMBLANCE TO THE ENDEARING IMAGES FAMILIAR FROM POPULAR CULTURE. YET EVEN IN THE ANCIENT JEWISH TRADITION, CHERUBIM WERE A BELOVED SACRED DECORATION—THAT IS, IF THE BIBLICAL DESCRIPTION OF JERUSALEM'S TEMPLE IS ANY INDICATION (SEE 1 KINGS 6:23–35 AND 2 CHRONICLES 3:8–14; ALSO NOTE EXODUS 25:18–22).

CHERUBIM

The most likely reason for their popularity was that people believed cherubim—or "winged creatures" as they are sometimes called—supported the heavenly throne of God.

In the Bible, however, cherubim are more than just temple décor. According to the book of Genesis, just after the first man and first woman sinned and were cast out of the Garden of Eden, God assigned cherubim to guard the entrance to the garden in order to prevent Adam and Eve from returning (Genesis 3:24).

However, it is the prophet Ezekiel's encounter on the bank of the Chebar River that provides the most detailed description of cherubim and their most important responsibility (Ezekiel 1:1-28). The cherubim that Ezekiel saw were attendants to the throne of God. The throne was transported on four wheels, each of which was directed by a cherub. The cherubim, as described by Ezekiel, had two pairs of wings—one that pointed upward and one that covered their bodies. Underneath the wings, each

A READING FROM EZEKIEL 1:4-14

I saw a windstorm blowing in from the north. Lightning flashed from a huge cloud and lit up the whole sky with a dazzling brightness. The fiery center of the cloud was as shiny as polished metal, and in that center I saw what looked like four living creatures. They were somewhat like humans, except that each one had four faces and four wings. Their legs were straight, but their feet looked like the hoofs of calves and sparkled like bronze. Under each of their wings, these creatures had a human hand. The four creatures were standing back to back with the tips of their wings touching. They moved together in every direction, without turning their bodies.

Each creature had the face of a human in front, the face of a lion on the right side, the face of a bull on the left, and the face of an eagle in back. Two wings of each creature were spread out and touched the wings of the creatures on either side. The other two wings of each creature were folded against its body. The four living creatures went wherever the Spirit led them, and they moved together without turning their bodies, because each creature faced straight ahead. The creatures were glowing like hot coals, and I saw something like a flaming torch moving back and forth among them. Lightning flashed from the torch every time its flame blazed up. The creatures themselves moved as quickly as sparks jumping from a fire.

cherub had a pair of hands that looked like human hands. Each one also had four faces—the face of a man, an ox, a lion, and an eagle. Their feet looked like those of calves. They were hardly the stuff of romantic greeting cards.

Ezekiel had a second vision of God's throne and its attendants (*see* 10:1-17). The cherubim in this vision resembled those in the first, but this time they also were covered with eyes. According to Ezekiel, the sound of the angels' wings was thunderous and resembled the voice of God.

Christ in Majesty, Kokkinobaphos Master (12th century)

Seraphim Purifying the Lips of Isaiah, Spanish School, (12th century)

SERAPHIM

ONE OF THE BIBLE'S MOST FAMOUS PROPHETS, ISAIAH, RECORDED IN VIVID DETAIL SEEING A VISION OF GOD'S THRONE SURROUNDED BY "FLAMING CREATURES" WITH SIX WINGS EACH, OTHERWISE KNOWN AS SERAPHIM (ISAIAH 6:1–8).

According to Isaiah, the remarkable creatures had six wings—a pair covering their faces, another pair covering their bodies, and yet a third pair, which they used to fly. In addition to the wings, the creatures that Isaiah saw may have had arms and hands of some kind, because one of the seraphim used a pair of tongs to seize a burning coal from the temple's altar and place it on Isaiah's mouth.

According to Isaiah's vision, the seraphim were attendants to God's heavenly throne. Their proximity to God has led some

"Holy, holy, holy, LORD All-Powerful! The earth is filled with your glory."

to suggest that seraphim sit at the top of the angelic hierarchy, followed closely by the cherubim. As depicted by Isaiah, one of their key roles seems to be audibly praising God as they circle the throne. The sound they produce, he declared, was so loud that it shook the celestial temple (Isaiah 6:4).

Isaiah's vision is the only direct reference to seraphim in Scripture. However, some believe that the six-winged creatures mentioned in the book of Revelation are synonymous with Isaiah's seraphim. In Revelation, the angelic beings continually sing, "Holy, holy, holy is the Lord, the all-powerful God, who was and is and is coming!" (Revelation 4:8). The chant is striking in its similarity to the one Isaiah heard in his vision.

The Voice of the Angels

Revelation 4–5 paints a glorious vision of worship in which angels, among other beings, honor God and the Lamb with words of praise. Revelation 5:11–12 includes an angelic refrain that is still used today in the liturgies of many churches, including Protestant, Catholic, and Orthodox. In this way, the "voice" of the angels in this vision extends through the centuries.

As I looked, I heard the voices of a large number of angels around the throne and the voices of the living creatures and of the elders. There were millions and millions of them, and they were saying in a loud voice, "The Lamb who was killed is worthy to receive power, riches, wisdom, strength, honor, glory, and praise."
– Revelation 5:11–12

A READING FROM ISAIAH 6:1–8

In the year that King Uzziah died, I had a vision of the LORD. He was on his throne high above, and his robe filled the temple. Flaming creatures with six wings each were flying over him. They covered their faces with two of their wings and their bodies with two more. They used the other two wings for flying, as they shouted,

"Holy, holy, holy, LORD All-Powerful! The earth is filled with your glory."

As they shouted, the doorposts of the temple shook, and the temple was filled with smoke. Then I cried out, "I'm doomed! Everything I say is sinful, and so are the words of everyone around me. Yet I have seen the King, the LORD All-Powerful."

One of the flaming creatures flew over to me with a burning coal that it had taken from the altar with a pair of metal tongs. It touched my lips with the hot coal and said, "This has touched your lips. Your sins are forgiven, and you are no longer guilty."

After this, I heard the LORD ask, "Is there anyone I can send? Will someone go for us?"

"I'll go," I answered. "Send me!"

above: *Adoration of the Mystic Lamb*, Jan van Eyck

THE ANGELS OF REVELATION

THE ANGELS DESCRIBED IN THE BOOK OF REVELATION ARE AMONG THE MOST IMPRESSIVE AND FRIGHTENING OF THOSE DESCRIBED IN THE BIBLE.

Revelation begins with an angel's appearance to John (Revelation 1:1). Later, John receives a second visitation from an angel who brings him "a little scroll" containing an apocalyptic vision (Revelation 10:1-11).

The angels that receive the most attention in Revelation are those who carry out God's judgment on the earth. John's book describes seven acts of judgment, each of which is initiated by an angel blowing a trumpet.

The trumpet-wielding angels are followed by a second group of angels who warn the people of earth about the impending judgment facing those who refuse to turn from evil (Revelation 14). Once the warnings cease, seven more angels arrive to deliver God's final judgments on the world in the form of terrifying plagues.

The angel I had seen standing on the sea and the land then held his right hand up toward heaven.

The archangel Michael's role as protector is highlighted in the story of the woman and the dragon in Revelation 12. When a war breaks out in heaven, it is Michael and his angels who fight against a red dragon with his own angel army.

One last angel from Revelation deserves mention. Near the end of John's book, we read about an angel who is sent to bind up "that old snake, who is also known as the devil and Satan" (20:2-3). The angels of Revelation seem to play an important role in the cosmic battle between good and evil.

The Angel of Revelation, William Blake (1757–1827)

A READING FROM REVELATION 14:6-20

I saw another angel. This one was flying across the sky and had the eternal good news to announce to the people of every race, tribe, language, and nation on earth. The angel shouted, "Worship and honor God! The time has come for him to judge everyone. Kneel down before the one who created heaven and earth, the oceans, and every stream."

A second angel followed and said, "The great city of Babylon has fallen! This is the city that made all nations drunk and immoral. Now God is angry, and Babylon has fallen."

Finally, a third angel came and shouted: "Here is what will happen if you worship the beast and the idol and have the mark of the beast on your hand or forehead. You will have to drink the wine that God gives to everyone who makes him angry. You will feel his mighty anger, and you will be tortured with fire and burning sulfur, while the holy angels and the Lamb look on.

If you worship the beast and the idol and accept the mark of its name, you will be tortured day and night. The smoke from your torture will go up forever and ever, and you will never be able to rest.

God's people must learn to endure. They must also obey his commands and have faith in Jesus."

Then I heard a voice from heaven say, "Put this in writing. From now on, the Lord will bless everyone who has faith in him when they die."

The Spirit answered, "Yes, they will rest from their hard work, and they will be rewarded for what they have done."

I looked and saw a bright cloud, and someone who seemed to be the Son of Man was sitting on the cloud. He wore a gold crown on his head and held a sharp sickle in his hand. An angel came out of the temple and shouted, "Start cutting with your sickle! Harvest season is here, and all crops on earth are ripe." The one on the cloud swung his sickle and harvested the crops.

Another angel with a sharp sickle then came out of the temple in heaven. After this, an angel with power over fire came from the altar and shouted to the angel who had the sickle. He said, "All grapes on earth are ripe! Harvest them with your sharp sickle." The angel swung his sickle on earth and cut off its grapes. He threw them into a pit where they were trampled on as a sign of God's anger. The pit was outside the city, and when the grapes were mashed, blood flowed out. The blood turned into a river that was about 200 miles long and almost deep enough to cover a horse.

The Last Judgment
Hans Memling (c.1433–1494)

READ IT FOR YOURSELF

EXODUS 23:20–23

I am sending an angel to protect you and to lead you into the land I have ready for you. Carefully obey everything the angel says, because I am giving him complete authority, and he won't tolerate rebellion. If you faithfully obey him, I will be a fierce enemy of your enemies. My angel will lead you into the land of the Amorites, Hittites, Perizzites, Canaanites, Hivites, and Jebusites, and I will wipe them out.

ANGELIC
ENCOUNTERS

DEPICTIONS OF ANGELS ARE ABUNDANT IN CONTEMPORARY CULTURE, WHERE THEY
INSPIRE MUCH CURIOSITY AND WONDER. THE MERCHANDISING OF ANGELS IS EVERY-
WHERE—FROM GARDEN STATUES TO GREETING CARDS, FROM COSTUMES TO TATTOOS,
AND MORE. AND ANGELS HAVE BEEN FAMILIAR CHARACTERS IN MOVIES AND TV
SHOWS FOR DECADES NOW: THE LUMPISH CLARENCE FROM "IT'S A WONDERFUL LIFE";
THE SOMETIMES SOMBER, SOMETIMES SASSY CAST OF "TOUCHED BY AN ANGEL";
JOHN TRAVOLTA'S IRREVERENT "MICHAEL"; AND THE BEER-SWILLING, TOBACCO-
CHEWING EARL IN "SAVING GRACE," TO NAME BUT A FEW. THANKS IN PART TO MADISON
AVENUE AND HOLLYWOOD, THE VERY DEFINITION OF ANGELIC HAS COME TO MEAN
"ADORABLE," "CUTE."

Not so the angels of Scripture: they could be
creatures of fierce power and strong presence.
Sometimes people trembled and sometimes they
ran when they saw angels—even people who
were accustomed to interacting with God. Often,
the first thing an angel had to say to a human was
something like, "Don't be so scared. Get up!"
Other times, angels appeared more or less as
guests or travelers, for example, in the story of
Abraham at Mamre (Genesis 18:1-15).

Indeed, angels were God's messengers, and they
were not dispatched to impart trivial news or
perform menial tasks. To encounter an angel
meant that God was about to communicate
critical information, to deliver someone from
a powerful threat, or perhaps to pass divine
judgment on a sinner.

In the stories that follow, angels presage the fiery
destruction of Sodom and Gomorrah, wrestle
in the dirt with a self-involved patriarch, hover
in midair with full intent to destroy Jerusalem,
aid and abet a prison escape, and convince
many to believe (and act on) what some might
consider impossible. Angels provided the birth
announcements for Isaac, Samson, John the
Baptist, and his relative, Jesus. They informed and
encouraged the believers after Jesus' death and
resurrection. In performing each of these tasks,
they were forceful representatives of God.

In fact, in many of these stories it can be difficult
to differentiate between God's messenger and God.
The angel may do the talking, but the recipient
of the message clearly interprets the words as
coming from God. Often, to encounter an angel
was to experience the alarming and awe-inspiring
fear of God.

READ IT FOR YOURSELF

GENESIS 21:14–19

Early the next morning Abraham gave Hagar an animal skin full of water and some bread. Then he put the boy on her shoulder and sent them away. They wandered around in the desert near Beersheba, and after they had run out of water, Hagar put her son under a bush. Then she sat down a long way off, because she could not bear to watch him die. And she cried bitterly.

When God heard the boy crying, the angel of God called out to Hagar from heaven and said, "Hagar, why are you worried? Don't be afraid. I have heard your son crying. Help him up and hold his hand, because I will make him the father of a great nation." Then God let her see a well. So she went to the well and filled the skin with water, then gave some to her son.

Hagar and Ishmael
Jean-Charles Cazin (1841–1901)

Being female and unmarried provided little status or opportunity for success in the ancient world, so Hagar might seem an unlikely candidate for an angelic visitation. She was a slave belonging to Sarah (Sarai), Abraham's wife. God had promised Abraham a child, but after Sarah appeared unable to conceive, Hagar was called on to serve as a surrogate and became pregnant by Abraham. Her pregnancy created enmity between Hagar and her master; and when Sarah began to mistreat her, Hagar ran away. Alone in the desert, she encountered an angel who sent her back home, and Hagar considered the rendezvous no less than a vision of God himself.

Fourteen years later, Sarah had a child of her own with Abraham, at which time she sent Hagar and her teenage son, Ishmael, away. Hagar expected her boy would die in the wilderness, but again an angel appeared. The angel comforted her, promising that her child would prosper and showing her the location of a nearby well.

Hagar and Ishmael in the Wilderness, Karel Dujardin

HAGAR

And an Angel of Provision and Promise

A Reading from Genesis 16:4-16

Later, when Hagar knew she was going to have a baby, she became proud and treated Sarai hatefully. Then Sarai said to Abram, "It's all your fault! I gave you my slave woman, but she has been hateful to me ever since she found out she was pregnant. You have done me wrong, and you will have to answer to the LORD for this." Abram said, "All right! She's your slave—do whatever you want with her." Then Sarai began treating Hagar so harshly that she finally ran away.

Hagar stopped to rest at a spring in the desert on the road to Shur. While she was there, the angel of the LORD came to her and asked, "Hagar, where have you come from, and where are you going?"

She answered, "I'm running away from Sarai, my owner."

The angel said, "Go back to Sarai and be her slave. I will give you a son, who will be called Ishmael, because I have heard your cry for help. And someday I will give you so many descendants that no one will be able to count them all. But your son will live far from his relatives; he will be like a wild donkey, fighting everyone, and everyone fighting him." Hagar thought, "Have I really seen God and lived to tell about it?" So from then on she called him, "The God Who Sees Me." That's why people call the well between Kadesh and Bered, "The Well of the Living One Who Sees Me." Abram was 86 years old when Hagar gave birth to their son, and he named him Ishmael.

Lot was Abraham's nephew, and he accompanied his uncle from Mesopotamia to Canaan. Once there, however, the scarcity of pasture for the two men's large flocks created friction between their herdsmen, so uncle and nephew agreed to part ways. Lot chose to move his flock to the well-watered plain of the Jordan, which also happened to be home to the infamous cities of Sodom and Gomorrah.

Lot's angelic encounter occurred just prior to God's destruction of the two cities. Neither the reluctance of Lot's family to leave their comfortable home nor the belligerent crowd's zeal for illicit sexual activity proved to be a problem for the two messengers sent by God. First, the visiting angels simply struck the hostile crowd blind. Then, when Lot and his family still hesitated at the thought of leaving, the angels took hold of the unresponsive humans and dragged them out of the city. As the fleeing group made their way toward safety in the nearby town of Zoar, Lot's wife defied the angels' order not to look back, and she suffered a grave consequence as a result. The instructions of the angels—who spoke for God—were not to be taken lightly.

The Destruction of Sodom and Gomorrah
John Martin, 1852

LOT

And Two Angels of Forewarning and Protection

A Reading from Genesis 19:1-26 (excerpted)

That evening, while Lot was sitting near the city gate, the two angels arrived in Sodom. When Lot saw them, he got up, bowed down low, and said, "Gentlemen, I am your servant. Please come to my home. You can wash your feet, spend the night, and be on your way in the morning." They told him, "No, we'll spend the night in the city square." But Lot kept insisting, until they finally agreed and went home with him. He quickly baked some bread, cooked a meal, and they ate. Before Lot and his guests could go to bed, every man in Sodom, young and old, came and stood outside his house and started shouting, "Where are your visitors? Send them out, so we can have sex with them!"...

The crowd kept arguing with Lot. Finally, they rushed toward the door to break it down. But the two angels in the house reached out and pulled Lot safely inside. Then they struck blind everyone in the crowd, and none of them could even find the door.

The two angels said to Lot, "The LORD has heard many terrible things about the people of Sodom, and he has sent us here to destroy the city. Take your family and leave. Take every relative you have in the city, as well as the men your daughters are going to marry." Lot went to the men who were engaged to his daughters and said, "Hurry up and get out of here! The LORD is going to destroy this city." But they thought he was joking, and they laughed at him.

Early the next morning the two angels tried to make Lot hurry and leave. They said, "Take your wife and your two daughters and get away from here as fast as you can! If you don't, every one of you will be killed when the LORD destroys the city." At first, Lot just stood there. But the LORD wanted to save him. So the angels took Lot, his wife, and his two daughters by the hand and led them out of the city. When they were outside, one of the angels said, "Run for your lives! Don't even look back. And don't stop in the valley. Run to the hills, where you'll be safe."

The sun was coming up as Lot reached the town of Zoar, and the LORD sent burning sulfur down like rain on Sodom and Gomorrah. He destroyed those cities and everyone who lived in them, as well as their land and the trees and grass that grew there.

On the way, Lot's wife looked back and was turned into a block of salt.

Angel of Sodom
Gustave Moreau (1826–1898)

Jacob Wrestling with the Angel
Alexandre-Louis Leloir (1843–1884)

READ IT FOR YOURSELF

GENESIS 32:24B-30

A man came and fought with Jacob until just before daybreak. When the man saw that he could not win, he struck Jacob on the hip and threw it out of joint. They kept on wrestling until the man said, "Let go of me! It's almost daylight."

"You can't go until you bless me," Jacob replied.

Then the man asked, "What is your name?" "Jacob," he answered.

The man said, "From now on, your name will no longer be Jacob. You will be called Israel, because you have wrestled with God and with men, and you have won." Jacob said, "Now tell me your name."

"Don't you know who I am?" he asked. And he blessed Jacob.

Jacob said, "I have seen God face to face, and I am still alive." So he named the place Peniel.

JACOB

And an Angel of Redirection and Renewal

Jacob was Abraham's grandson, the son of Isaac. He would come to be known as Israel, and his children would be the progenitors of the twelve tribes.

But throughout most of Jacob's early life, he was a trickster or con man. His manipulative acquisition of his brother Esau's birthright and blessing met with murderous threats from Esau. Ultimately, Jacob had to leave home for his own protection (Genesis 27:41-45). While away, he matched wits with his uncle Laban (his mother's brother) for a couple of decades before returning home. During this period of transition—first

leaving home, then returning— he had two encounters with angels.

The first was a dream in which angels ascended and descended a "ladder," or "staircase," that reached all the way to heaven. The experience left him with the realization that he wasn't solely in charge of his life—a vision that perhaps proved both unsettling and reassuring all at once.

Twenty years later, on his way home to meet Esau, Jacob took part in an all-night wrestling match with an unidentified "man." Though this figure was not clearly identified in the Genesis account, the prophet

Hosea later referred to him as an angel (Hosea 12:3-4). Jacob, however, considered the experience a "face-to-face" encounter with God. (His name for the location, Peniel, meant "face of God." *See* Genesis 32:30.) Even after realizing that he was no match for his opponent, the ever-persistent Jacob would not walk away empty-handed. He refused to release the mysterious figure until he had received a blessing. The unidentified man announced that henceforth Jacob would be known as "Israel," which may mean "a man who wrestles with God."

GIDEON

And an Angel of Counsel and Courage

During an era when judges ruled over Israel, the people underwent a recurring cycle of spiritual ups and downs. First they would turn away from God, becoming spiritually weak, a condition that would leave them politically weak as well. Soon they would fall into subjection to one of their enemies. Then, once they had lost their freedom, they would turn back to God. Eventually, a national champion—or judge —would rise up and, with God's power, help the people defeat their enemies.

While some judges were natural leaders, Gideon was anything but that. When we first meet Gideon, he is trying to thresh some grain in an unlikely (and inconvenient) area. Gideon, it turns out, was trying to avoid confrontation with the very enemies God wanted him to fight. The unlikely hero would go on to defeat the numerous and powerful Midianites using a weaponless army of only three hundred men (Judges 7). But it all began with a perplexing visit by an angel, a miraculous, convincing sign, and a decision to believe (however reluctantly) in the angel's assessment of his capabilities as a leader.

Gideon and the Fleece
French School (15th century)

READ IT FOR YOURSELF

JUDGES 6:11–14

One day an angel from the LORD went to the town of Ophrah and sat down under the big tree that belonged to Joash, a member of the Abiezer clan. Joash's son Gideon was nearby, threshing grain in a shallow pit, where he could not be seen by the Midianites.

The angel appeared and spoke to Gideon, "The LORD is helping you, and you are a strong warrior."

Gideon answered, "Please don't take this wrong, but if the LORD is helping us, then why have all of these awful things happened? We've heard how the LORD performed miracles and rescued our ancestors from Egypt. But those things happened long ago. Now the LORD has abandoned us to the Midianites."

Then the LORD himself said, "Gideon, you will be strong, because I am giving you the power to rescue Israel from the Midianites."

PRENATAL ANGELIC INSTRUCTION

JUST AS GIDEON BEFORE HIM, SAMSON SERVED AS ONE OF THE JUDGES OF ISRAEL. SAMSON'S LONG LOCKS OF HAIR, AND HIS STRENGTH ASSOCIATED WITH THAT HAIR, ARE A WELL-KNOWN PART OF HIS STORY. LESSER KNOWN IS THE FACT THAT AN ANGELIC APPEARANCE PREPARED SAMSON'S PARENTS FOR HIS BIRTH AND OFFERED INSTRUCTIONS FOR THE RAISING OF THEIR SON.

THE ANGEL—REFERRED TO AS AN "ANGEL FROM THE LORD"—APPEARED FIRST TO SAMSON'S MOTHER BEFORE SHE WAS WITH CHILD. HE ANNOUNCED HER UPCOMING PREGNANCY AND PLACED SOME VERY SPECIFIC DEMANDS—FOR BOTH HER PREGNANCY AND FOR SAMSON'S LIFESTYLE. THEN, AT THE REQUEST OF MANOAH, SOON-TO-BE SAMSON'S FATHER, THE ANGEL RETURNED. HE CONFIRMED HIS INSTRUCTIONS AND FIELDED MANOAH'S QUESTIONS.

AT FIRST, MANOAH VIEWED HIS VISITOR AS MERELY A MAN, BUT THEN, AT THE ANGEL'S SUGGESTION, MANOAH OFFERED A SACRIFICE. THE SACRIFICE WAS MIRACULOUSLY CONSUMED AND THE ANGEL RETURNED TO HEAVEN. HAVING WITNESSED THESE EVENTS, MANOAH REALIZED HE HAD BEEN IN THE PRESENCE OF ONE OF THE LORD'S ANGELS.

An Angel Announces the Birth of Samson
to the Barren Wife of Manoah
Nicholas of Verdun (c.1150–1205)

A Reading from Judges 13:1-25

Once again the Israelites started disobeying the LORD. So he let the Philistines take control of Israel for 40 years.

Manoah from the tribe of Dan lived in the town of Zorah. His wife was not able to have children, but one day an angel from the LORD appeared to her and said:

"You have never been able to have any children, but very soon you will be pregnant and have a son. He will belong to God from the day he is born, so his hair must never be cut. And even before he is born, you must not drink any wine or beer or eat any food forbidden by God's laws.

Your son will begin to set Israel free from the Philistines."

She went to Manoah and said, "A prophet who looked like an angel of God came and talked to me. I was so frightened, that I didn't even ask where he was from. He didn't tell me his name, but he did say that I'm going to have a baby boy. I'm not supposed to drink any wine or beer or eat any food forbidden by God's laws. Our son will belong to God for as long as he lives."

Then Manoah prayed, "Our LORD, please send that prophet again and let him tell us what to do for the son we are going to have."

God answered Manoah's prayer, and the angel went back to Manoah's wife while she was resting in the fields. Manoah wasn't there at the time, so she found him and said, "That same man is here again! He's the one I saw the other day."

Manoah went with his wife and asked the man, "Are you the one who spoke to my wife?" "Yes, I am," he answered. Manoah then asked, "When your promise comes true, what rules must he obey and what will be his work?" "Your wife must be careful to do everything I told her," the LORD's angel answered.

"She must not eat or drink anything made from grapes. She must not drink wine or beer or eat anything forbidden by God's laws. I told her exactly what to do."

"Please," Manoah said, "stay here with us for just a little while, and we'll fix a young goat for you to eat."

Manoah didn't realize that he was really talking to one of the LORD's angels.

The angel answered, "I can stay for a little while, although I won't eat any of your food. But if you would like to offer the goat as a sacrifice to the LORD, that would be fine."

Manoah said, "Tell us your name, so we can honor you after our son is born."

"No," the angel replied. "You don't need to know my name. And if you did, you couldn't understand it."

So Manoah took a young goat over to a large rock he had chosen for an altar, and he built a fire on the rock. Then he killed the goat, and offered it with some grain as a sacrifice to the LORD. But then an amazing thing happened.

The fire blazed up toward the sky, and the LORD's angel went up toward heaven in the fire. Manoah and his wife bowed down low when they saw what happened.

Although the angel didn't appear to them again, they realized he was one of the LORD's angels.

Manoah said, "We have seen an angel. Now we're going to die."

"The LORD isn't going to kill us," Manoah's wife responded. "The LORD accepted our sacrifice and grain offering, and he let us see something amazing. Besides, he told us that we're going to have a son."

Later, Manoah's wife did give birth to a son, and she named him Samson. As the boy grew, the LORD blessed him.

Then, while Samson was staying at Dan's Camp between the towns of Zorah and Eshtaol, the Spirit of the LORD took control of him.

Many people know about David's triumph over Goliath, his rise and reign as Israel's most famous king, and his shocking affair with Bathsheba and murder of her husband in an attempt to cover his indiscretion. Perhaps less known is David's experience with one of the most terrifying angels in the Bible.

DAVID
And an Angel of Counsel and Courage

Late in his career, David conducted a census of his troops—in an incident that was attributed to Satan's influence (1 Chronicles 21:1). The act in itself was not improper, but David's motives were suspect and his ordering the census made God angry.

After being allowed to choose his own punishment, David saw an angel of destruction—who was witnessed by others as well—poised in midair, ready to destroy Jerusalem, the capital city of Israel. Seventy thousand people had already died across Israel. In his mercy, however, God withheld the angel's hand, and Jerusalem was spared.

A Reading from 1 Chronicles 21:7-30 (excerpted)

David's order to count the people made God angry, and he punished Israel. David prayed, "I am your servant. But what I did was stupid and terribly wrong. Please forgive me."

The LORD said to Gad, one of David's prophets, "Tell David that I will punish him in one of three ways. But he will have to choose which one it will be."

Gad went to David and told him: "You must choose how the LORD will punish you: Will there be three years when the land won't grow enough food for its people? Or will your enemies constantly defeat you for three months? Or will the LORD send a horrible disease to strike your land for three days? Think about it and decide, because I have to give your answer to God who sent me."

David was miserable and said, "It's a terrible choice to make! But the LORD is kind, and I'd rather be punished by him than by anyone else."

So the LORD sent a horrible disease on Israel, and 70,000 Israelites died. Then he sent an angel to destroy the city of Jerusalem. But just as the angel was about to do that, the LORD felt sorry for all the suffering he had caused the people, and he told the angel, "Stop! They have suffered enough." This happened at the threshing place that belonged to Araunah the Jebusite. David saw the LORD's angel in the air, holding a sword over Jerusalem. He and the leaders of Israel, who were all wearing sackcloth, bowed with their faces to the ground, and David prayed, "It's my fault! I sinned by ordering the people to be counted. They have done nothing wrong— they are innocent sheep. LORD God, please punish me and my family. Don't let the disease wipe out your people."

The LORD's angel told the prophet Gad to tell David that he must go to Araunah's threshing place and build an altar in honor of the LORD. David followed the LORD's instructions.

Just then, David arrived, and when Araunah saw him, he stopped his work and bowed down.... Araunah and his four sons were threshing wheat at the time, and when they saw the angel, the four sons ran to hide. So David paid Araunah 600 gold coins for his threshing place. David built an altar and offered sacrifices to please the LORD and sacrifices to ask his blessing. David prayed, and the LORD answered him by sending fire down on the altar. Then the LORD commanded the angel to put the sword away. When David saw that the LORD had answered his prayer, he offered more sacrifices there at the threshing place, because he was afraid of the angel's sword and did not want to go all the way to Gibeon. That's where the sacred tent that Moses had made in the desert was kept, as well as the altar where sacrifices were offered to the LORD.

Donatello's *David* shows David at the time of his defeat of Goliath (c.1386–1466)

Daniel, the young man who was carried to Babylon with a number of captive Israelites, is well-known for experiencing a dramatic deliverance by God's hand. His friends Shadrach, Meshach, and Abednego were miraculously spared from the intense flames of the fiery furnace (Daniel 3), and Daniel himself survived a night in a den full of hungry lions when God intervened, shutting their mouths (Daniel 6). Both events refer to an angel who was sent to protect God's faithful servants (3:28; 6:22).

However, the book of Daniel also contains less familiar tales in which the prophet conversed with angels (or "holy ones") in dreams or visions. Two such angels are identified by name: Gabriel (8:16; 9:21) and Michael (10:13, 21; 12:1). One passage describes a heavenly battle between angels, so severe that an angel on the way to see Daniel was detained for three weeks. In order to complete his mission and deliver his message to Daniel, the angel needed to enlist even more powerful help—that of Michael the archangel.

In this instance, Daniel saw the angel in a vision. The angel did not bear bad news—but instead came to bring insight and peace.

Upon seeing this messenger from God, Daniel was nonetheless rendered helpless. The people who accompanied Daniel at the time were not able to see his actual vision, yet they were inexplicably terrified, and they ran and hid.

DANIEL

And An Angel with Answers and Assurance

A Reading from Daniel 10:2–19

Daniel wrote: For three weeks I was in sorrow. I ate no fancy food or meat, I drank no wine, and I put no olive oil on my face or hair. Then, on the twenty-fourth day of the first month, I was standing on the banks of the great Tigris River, when I looked up and saw someone dressed in linen and wearing a solid gold belt. His body was like a precious stone, his face like lightning, his eyes like flaming fires, his arms and legs like polished bronze, and his voice like the roar of a crowd. Although the people who were with me did not see the vision, they became so frightened that they scattered and hid. Only I saw this great vision. I became weak and pale, and at the sound of his voice, I fell facedown in a deep sleep. He raised me to my hands and knees and then said, "Daniel, your God thinks highly of you, and he has sent me. So stand up and pay close attention." I stood trembling, while the angel said:

"Daniel, don't be afraid! God has listened to your prayers since the first day you humbly asked for understanding, and he has sent me here. But the guardian angel of Persia opposed me for 21 days. Then Michael, who is one of the strongest guardian angels, came to rescue me from the kings of Persia. Now I have come here to give you another vision about what will happen to your people in the future."

While this angel was speaking to me, I stared at the ground, speechless. Then he appeared in human form and touched my lips. I said, "Sir, this vision has brought me great pain and has drained my strength. I am merely your servant. How can I possibly speak with someone so powerful, when I am almost too weak to get my breath?"

The angel touched me a second time and said, "Don't be frightened! God thinks highly of you, and he intends this for your good, so be brave and strong."

At this, I regained my strength and replied, "Please speak! You have already made me feel much better."

Daniel's Answer to the King, Briton Rivière

Angels appear at key points in the biblical accounts of the life and times of Jesus. Prior to his birth, God sent an angel to inform a priest named Zechariah that he and his wife Elizabeth would have a son (John the Baptist), who would prepare his people for the arrival of their Messiah.

Imagine Zechariah's unsettled reaction when, while performing his quiet and solitary duties in the temple, he suddenly sensed that he wasn't alone. His terror grew when he realized his visitor was an angel. Zechariah and his wife Elizabeth had been devout in their faith for many years, but now they were elderly yet remained childless. The angel's news was wonderful and, frankly, unbelievable: Elizabeth was going to have a baby.

Considering their advanced ages, it seems difficult to blame Zechariah for being a bit skeptical. Still, because of his initial doubt, the angel rendered him speechless until the birth of the promised child. After John was born, the first words out of Zechariah's mouth were spoken in praise to God (Luke 1:62-64, 67-79).

ZECHARIAH
And An Angel of Unexpected Bounty and Blessing

A Reading from Luke 1:8-20

One day Zechariah's group of priests were on duty, and he was serving God as a priest. According to the custom of the priests, he had been chosen to go into the Lord's temple that day and to burn incense, while the people stood outside praying. All at once an angel from the Lord appeared to Zechariah at the right side of the altar. Zechariah was confused and afraid when he saw the angel. But the angel told him:

"Don't be afraid, Zechariah! God has heard your prayers. Your wife Elizabeth will have a son, and you must name him John. His birth will make you very happy, and many people will be glad. Your son will be a great servant of the Lord. He must never drink wine or beer, and the power of the Holy Spirit will be with him from the time he is born.

John will lead many people in Israel to turn back to the Lord their God. He will go ahead of the Lord with the same power and spirit that Elijah had. And because of John, parents will be more thoughtful of their children. And people who now disobey God will begin to think as they ought to. This is how John will get people ready for the Lord."

Zechariah said to the angel, "How will I know this is going to happen? My wife and I are both very old."

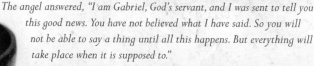

The angel answered, "I am Gabriel, God's servant, and I was sent to tell you this good news. You have not believed what I have said. So you will not be able to say a thing until all this happens. But everything will take place when it is supposed to."

An Angel Tells Zechariah That He Will Have a Son
Mosaic. 14th c.
Baptistery, Venice, Italy

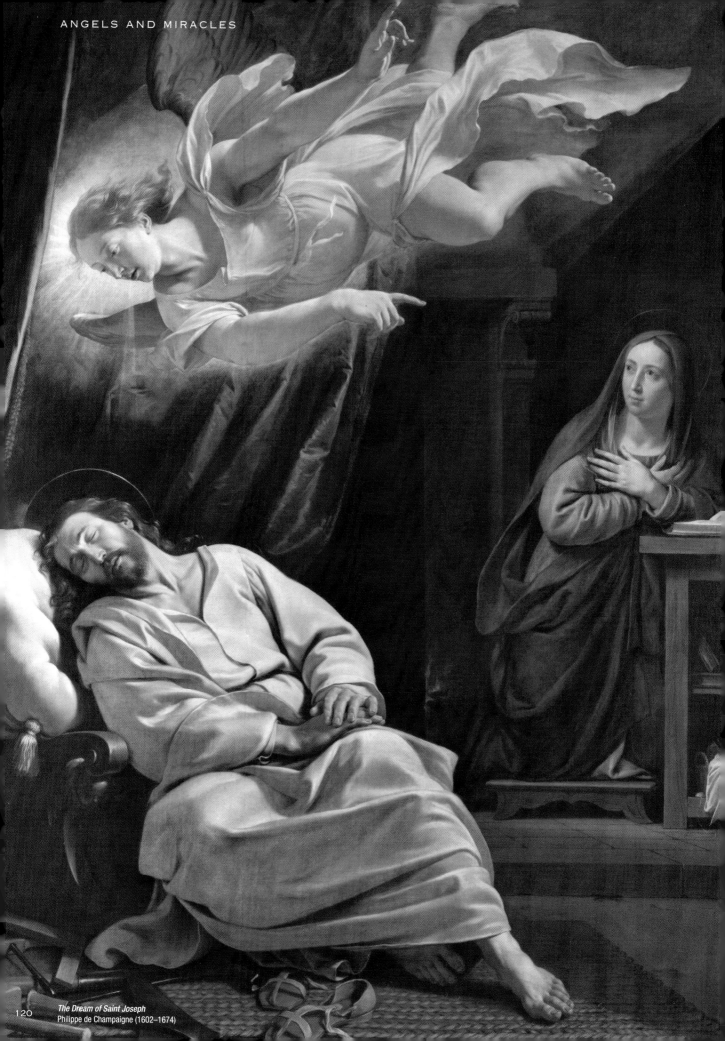

The Dream of Saint Joseph
Philippe de Champaigne (1602–1674)

God prepared to enter the world in human form as the child of a simple carpenter and a humble young girl. The angel Gabriel delivered the startling news to Mary first. She was understandably bewildered at how she could possibly give birth, since she was a virgin, yet she submitted to the will of God.

MARY AND JOSEPH

And an Angel of Challenge and Change

A Reading from Matthew 1:18-25

This is how Jesus Christ was born. A young woman named Mary was engaged to Joseph from King David's family. But before they were married, she learned that she was going to have a baby by God's Holy Spirit. Joseph was a good man and did not want to embarrass Mary in front of everyone. So he decided to quietly call off the wedding. While Joseph was thinking about this, an angel from the Lord came to him in a dream. The angel said, "Joseph, the baby that Mary will have is from the Holy Spirit. Go ahead and marry her. Then after her baby is born, name him Jesus, because he will save his people from their sins." So the Lord's promise came true, just as the prophet had said, "A virgin will have a baby boy, and he will be called Immanuel," which means "God is with us."

After Joseph woke up, he and Mary were soon married, just as the Lord's angel had told him to do. But they did not sleep together before her baby was born. Then Joseph named him Jesus.

When Joseph learned of Mary's pregnancy, he knew it wasn't his child, and he decided to end their relationship quietly. To his credit, his chief desire was to spare Mary from being the object of local gossip and humiliation. But when an angel then appeared to Joseph in a dream to assure him that Mary had done nothing improper, Joseph decided to take Mary as his wife after all. As a result, the two of them proved instrumental in fulfilling a centuries-old promise of God's redemption.

Later, Mary and Joseph protected the infant Jesus from the wrath of King Herod, fleeing their home for the safety of Egypt. Angels directed the couple, telling them when to leave and when to return (Matthew 2:13-23).

Angels Among Us

Most major religions acknowledge angelic beings, and many see angels as ways to connect with the divine. But even outside of religious circles, angels continue to be a popular topic.

It might be true that this cultural fascination with angels hints at some desire for God. It may even speak to the hope that if we face the reality of God's existence, we hope we can encounter him in such a way that neither his presence nor his power will terrify us.

After Jesus' death, resurrection, and return to heaven, the Holy Spirit arrived to comfort and empower his followers (Acts 2). During Jesus' trial and execution, even those closest to him had been guilty of betraying, denying, and deserting him. Yet now, with the Holy Spirit to help, they began to speak and act with boldness. Very soon, their audacity met with resistance, and Peter found himself imprisoned. Even so, he was sleeping soundly when he had an angelic encounter in the depths of his jail. (The angel had to physically poke him to wake him up!)

In this instance, only Peter was aware of the angel's presence. In fact, he thought he was dreaming at first. It was only after he found himself on the street, alone and free, that he realized the experience was indeed genuine. He wasn't the only one surprised, either; when he arrived at a home filled with friends who were praying for his release, it took some time for them to believe it was really Peter (Acts 12:12-16).

PETER

And an Angel of Release and Rescue

A Reading from Acts 12:1-16

At that time King Herod caused terrible suffering for some members of the church. He ordered soldiers to cut off the head of James, the brother of John. When Herod saw that this pleased the Jewish people, he had Peter arrested during the Festival of Thin Bread. He put Peter in jail and ordered four squads of soldiers to guard him. Herod planned to put him on trial in public after the festival. While Peter was being kept in jail, the church never stopped praying to God for him.

The night before Peter was to be put on trial, he was asleep and bound by two chains. A soldier was guarding him on each side, and two other soldiers were guarding the entrance to the jail. Suddenly an angel from the Lord appeared, and light flashed around in the cell. The angel poked Peter in the side and woke him up. Then he said, "Quick! Get up!"

The chains fell off his hands, and the angel said, "Get dressed and put on your sandals." Peter did what he was told. Then the angel said, "Now put on your coat and follow me." Peter left with the angel, but he thought everything was only a dream. They went past the two groups of soldiers, and when they came to the iron gate to the city, it opened by itself. They went out and were going along the street, when all at once the angel disappeared.

Peter now realized what had happened, and he said, "I am certain that the Lord sent his angel to rescue me from Herod and from everything the Jewish leaders planned to do to me." Then Peter went to the house of Mary the mother of John whose other name was Mark. Many of the Lord's followers had come together there and were praying.

Peter knocked on the gate, and a servant named Rhoda came to answer. When she heard Peter's voice, she was too excited to open the gate. She ran back into the house and said that Peter was standing there.

"You are crazy!" everyone told her. But she kept saying that it was Peter. Then they said, "It must be his angel." But Peter kept on knocking, until finally they opened the gate. They saw him and were completely amazed.

The Liberation of St. Peter
Alessandro Turchi (1579–1649)

EPILOGUE
Eyes for the Miraculous

As people living in a postmodern culture, we tend to face our obstacles and adversities without expecting them to disappear supernaturally. After all, we have practical resources. We have scientific understanding. We have advanced technology.

Yet the mysterious and the miraculous are always with us. Even though we understand much about how the world works—and perhaps, in part, as a reaction to this understanding—many of us hold a reverence for those things that are beyond our understanding. We remain aware of, and sometimes even enamored by, the unexplainable.

In these pages, we've looked at a variety of events that the biblical writers regarded as miraculous. It's important to remember, however, that the message of the Bible does not depend upon our ability to understand or explain these events. The biblical message assumes the fact that God is all-powerful and can act outside of what we think and know. The significance seems to lie not in the events themselves, but in the God who used them to capture people's attention and to provide hope for those who saw his works and believed in his power.

From an amazingly angelic appearance to an unlikely warrior granted exceptional abilities, these events are like a beacon or signal fire, drawing our attention to what matters most in the discussion—the timeless God who guides and cares for humanity.

A Reading from Hebrews 2:1-4

We must give our full attention to what we were told, so we won't drift away. The message spoken by angels proved to be true, and all who disobeyed or rejected it were punished as they deserved. So if we refuse this great way of being saved, how can we hope to escape? The Lord himself was the first to tell about it, and people who heard the message proved to us that it was true. God himself showed that his message was true by working all kinds of powerful miracles and wonders. He also gave his Holy Spirit to anyone he chose to.

READ IT FOR YOURSELF

ACTS 2:22
Now, listen to what I have to say about Jesus from Nazareth. God proved he sent Jesus to you by having him work miracles, wonders, and signs. All of you know this.

ACTS 6:8
God gave Stephen the power to work great miracles and wonders among the people.

SOURCES

Angels and Miracles is not intended to be a definitive source of information; rather it was written to invite you to explore for yourself the significance of the marvelous stories and truths that are contained in the Bible. As we compiled our research, we took great care to question and verify. Now, we offer you the opportunity to research and verify our findings as well, and we invite you to further explore these sources for yourself.

EDITORIAL SOURCES

The following resources were used to develop the material in this book.

❶ Books written on specific topics
❷ Bible dictionaries or encyclopedias with entries for people, places, and events
❸ Commentaries that explore the Bible text by sections of verses
❹ Credible online sources

BOOKS

- Erickson, Millard. 1998. *Christian Theology.* Baker Academic.
- Butler, Trent ed. 2003. *Holman Illustrated Bible Dictionary.* Broadman & Holman.
- *NIV Life Application Study Bible.* Zondervan. 2008.
- Lockyer, Herbert, ed. 1995. *All the Angels in the Bible: a complete exploration of the nature and ministry of angels.* Hendrickson Publishers.
- C.S. Lewis. 2001. *Miracles.* HarperOne.
- MacArthur, John. 2005. *The MacArthur Bible Commentary.* Thomas Nelson.
- *The Learning Bible.* American Bible Society. 2000.

ONLINE SOURCES

- amazingchange.org
- bible.org
- biblesearch.com
- christiananswers.net
- christianitytoday.com
- everystudent.com
- gotquestions.org
- lifeofchrist.com
- miraclesofthebible.com
- pantheon.org

ART SOURCES

ART RESOURCE

The Dream of Saint Joseph, 1642–3
Champaigne, Philippe de (1602–1674)
Location: National Gallery, London, Great Britain
Photo Credit: © National Gallery, London / Art Resource, NY

Abraham and the Three Angel, 1896–1902
Tissot, James Jacques Joseph (1836–1902)
Location: The Jewish Museum, New York, NY, U.S.A.
Photo Credit: The Jewish Museum, NY / Art Resource, NY

Angel of Sodom, 1837
Moreau, Gustave (1826-1898)
Location: Musee Gustave Moreau, Paris, France
Photo Credit: Réunion des Musées Nationaux / Art Resource, NY

An Angel Announces the Birth of Samson to the Barren Wife of Manoah
Nicholas of Verdun (c.1150-1205)
Location: Sammlungen des Stiftes, Klosterneuburg Abbey, Austria
Photo Credit: Erich Lessing / Art Resource, NY

An Angel Tells Zachariah That He Will Have a Son
Mosaic. 14th c.
Location: Baptistery, Venice, Italy
Photo Credit: Erich Lessing / Art Resource, NY

The Tomb of Lazarus at Jerusalem
Anonymous, 19th century
Location: Tomb of Lazarus, Bethany, Israel
Photo Credit: Adoc-photos / Art Resource, NY

The Prophet Elijah
Sassetta (Stefano di Giovanni) (c.1400–1450)
Location: Pinacoteca Nazionale, Siena, Italy
Photo Credit: Scala / Art Resource, NY

The Prophet Elisha
Sassetta (Stefano di Giovanni) (c.1400–1450)
Location : Pinacoteca Nazionale, Siena, Italy
Photo Credit : Scala / Art Resource, NY

The Taking of Jericho
Tissot, James Jacques Joseph (1836–1902)
Location: The Jewish Museum, New York, NY, U.S.A.
Photo Credit: The Jewish Museum, NY / Art Resource, NY

Elijah and the priest of Baal
Cranach, Lucas the Younger (1515–1586)
Location: Gemaeldegalerie Alte Meister, Staatliche Kunstsammlungen, Dresden, Germany
Photo Credit: Bildarchiv Preussischer Kulturbesitz / Art Resource, NY

The Three Angels Appearing to Abraham
Tiepolo, Giambattista (1696–1770)
Location: Accademia, Venice, Italy
Photo Credit: Cameraphoto Arte, Venice / Art Resource, NY

Shadrach, Meshach and Abednego, the Three Youths in the Fiery Furnace of Nebuchadnezzer
Byzantine Mosaic, 11th CE
Location: Monastery Church, Hosios Loukas, Greece
Photo Credit: Erich Lessing / Art Resource, NY

The Crossing of the Red Sea
Chagall, Marc (1887–1985) © ARS, NY
Location: Musee National message biblique Marc Chagall, Nice, France
Photo Credit: Réunion des Musées Nationaux / Art Resource, NY

Detail from "Spanish Actions Deflected by the Taking of Ghent"
Le Brun, Charles (1619–1690)
Location: Chateaux de Versailles et de Trianon, Versailles, France
Photo Credit: Réunion des Musées Nationaux / Art Resource, NY

Massacre of the Innocents
Pisano, Giovanni (1248–c.1314)
Location: Duomo, Pisa, Italy
Photo Credit: Scala / Art Resource, NY

Roman Jugs from Cana, Israel
Location: Studium Biblicum Franciscanum, Jerusalem, Israel
Photo Credit: Erich Lessing / Art Resource, NY

Early Morning in the Wilderness of Shur
Goodall, Frederick (1822–1904)
Location: Guildhall Art Gallery, London, Great Britain
Photo Credit: HIP / Art Resource, NY

Crossing of the Red Sea
Belbello da Pavia (c.1430–1473)
Location: Biblioteca Nazionale, Florence, Italy
Photo Credit: Scala / Art Resource, NY

The Burning of Sodom
Corot, Jean-Baptiste Camille (1796–1875)
Location: The Metropolitan Museum of Art, New York, NY, U.S.A.
Photo Credit: Image copyright © The Metropolitan Museum of Art / Art Resource, NY

The Fall of Nineveh
Martin, John (1789–1854)
Location: Victoria and Albert Museum, London, Great Britain
Photo Credit: Art Resource, NY

BRIDGEMAN

The Liberation of Saint Peter from Prison
Honthorst, Gerrit van (1590–1656)

Gideon and the Fleece, c.1490 (oil on panel), French School (15th century), Musee du Petit Palais, Avignon, France

Samson Slays the Lion, Francesco Hayez (1791–1882) Galleria d'Arte Moderna, Florence, Italy

The Ascension from the Mount of Olives, illustration for 'The Life of Christ', c.1884–96 Tissot, James Jacques Joseph (1836–1902)

David, c.1440 (bronze), Donatello, (c.1386–1466) Museo Nazionale del Bargello, Florence, Italy

Moses and the Brazen Serpent, 1618–1620 (oil on canvas) Sir Anthony van Dyck (1599–1641), Prado, Madrid, Spain

The Last Judgement, 1473 (oil on panel), Hans Memling (c.1433–1494), Muzeum Narodowe, Gdansk, Poland

Gabriel, 1991 (acrylic on canvas), Laura James (Contemporary Artist), Private Collection

Hagar and Ishmael, Jean-Charles Cazin (1841–1901) Musee des Beaux-Arts, Tours, France

Jacob Wrestling with the Angel, 1865 (oil on canvas) Alexandre-Louis Leloir (1843-84), Musee des Beaux-Arts, Clermont-Ferrand, France

The Liberation of St. Peter, Alessandro Turchi (1579–1649) Galleria e Museo Estense, Modena, Italy

Ms Grec 1208 f.162 Christ in Majesty, from Homilies on the Virgin, composed by James of Kokkinophabus (vellum) by Kokkinobaphos Master (12th century), Bibliotheque Nationale, Paris, France

Christ Glorified in the Court of Heaven, detail of musical angels from the right hand side, 1419-35 (tempera on panel) (detail of 4052), Fra Angelico (Guido di Pietro) (c.1387–1455) National Gallery, London, UK

Icon of the Archangel Michael, (egg tempera on panel) Egyptian School (18th century), Benaki Museum, Athens, Greece

And Then There was a Great Cry in Egypt, 1897 (oil on canvas) Arthur Hacker (1858–1919), Private Collection/The Fine Art Society, London, UK

The Angel of Revelation, c.1805 (w/c, pen & ink over graphite) William Blake (1757–1827), Metropolitan Museum of Art, New York, USA

Seraphim Purifying the Lips of Isaiah, Catalan School (fresco) Spanish School, (12th century), Museo de Arte de Catalunya, Barcelona, Spain

MISCELLANEOUS

120 Great Paintings of the Life of Christ, The Dore Bible Illustrations, Dore's Angels, Christian Art and Imagery
Dover

FotoSearch
www.fotosearch.com

Dreamstime
www.dreamstime.com

Jericho Mud Brick Wall, chapter 2
Todd Bolen
www.BiblePlaces.com

Wikipedia
Some images have been pulled from various Wikipedia resources and have been designated as public domain images because their copyright has expired.

All other images:
iStock Photo, www.istockphoto.com

HISTORY AND MISSION OF THE AMERICAN BIBLE SOCIETY

Since the establishment of the American Bible Society in 1816, its history has been closely intertwined with the history of the nation whose name it bears. In fact, the Society's early leadership reads like a Who's Who of patriots and other American movers and shakers. Its first president was Elias Boudinot, formerly the president of the Continental Congress. John Jay, John Quincy Adams, DeWitt Clinton, and chronicler of the new nation James Fenimore Cooper also played significant roles in the Society's history, as would Rutherford B. Hayes and Benjamin Harrison in later generations.

AMERICAN BIBLE SOCIETY

From the beginning, the Bible Society's mission has been to respond to the spiritual needs of a fast-growing, diverse population in a rapidly expanding nation. From the new frontier beyond the Appalachian Mountains, missionaries sent back dire reports of towns that did not have a single copy of the Bible to share among its citizens. State and local Bible societies did not have the resources, network, or capabilities to fill this growing need: a national organization was called for. The ABS committed itself to organizational and technological innovations to meet the demand. No longer subject to British restrictions, the ABS could set up its own printing plants, develop better qualities of paper and ink, and establish a network of colporteurs to get the Bibles to the people who needed them.

Reaching out to diverse audiences has always been at the heart of ABS's mission. Scriptures were made available to native peoples in their own languages —in Delaware in 1818, followed soon by Mohawk, Seneca, Ojibwa, Cherokee, and others. French and Spanish Bibles were published for the Louisiana Territory, Florida, and the Southwest. By the 1890s, the ABS was printing or distributing Scriptures in German, Portuguese, Chinese, Italian, Russian, Danish, Polish, Hungarian, Czech, and other languages to meet the spiritual needs of an increasing immigrant population. In 1836, 75 years before the first Braille Bibles were produced, the ABS was providing Scriptures to the blind in "raised letter" editions.

Responding to the need for Bibles in the languages and formats that speak most deeply to people's hearts continues to be a priority of the ABS. Through its partnerships with other national Bible Societies, the ABS can provide some portion of Scripture in almost any language that has a written form. It has also been able to provide Braille Scriptures for the blind as well as recorded Scriptures for the visually impaired, dyslexic, and people who have not yet learned to read.

The Bible Society's founders and their successors have always understood the Bible as a text that can speak to people's deepest needs in times of crisis. The ABS distributed its first Scriptures to the military in 1817, when it provided New Testaments to the crew of the USS *John Adams*, a frigate that had served in the War of 1812 and was continuing its service to the country by protecting the American coast from pirates. During the Civil War, the ABS provided Testaments to both northern and southern forces, and it has continued to provide Bibles and Testaments to the U.S. military forces during every subsequent war, conflict, and operation. During the painful post-Reconstruction era, when Jim Crow laws prevailed in many parts of the nation, the ABS was able to provide Scriptures to African Americans through its partnership with the Agency Among Colored People of the South and through the historic black churches.

This faith that the Word of God speaks in special ways during times of crisis continues to inform the ABS mission. In recent years, the Bible Society has produced Scripture booklets addressing the needs of people with HIV/AIDS and of those experiencing profound loss due to acts of terrorism and natural disasters.

Translation and scholarship are key components in the Bible Society's mission of communicating the Word of God faithfully and powerfully. In the mid-20th century, the ABS, in partnership with the United Bible Societies, developed innovative theories and practices of translation. First, they insisted that all the Bible translations they sponsored were to be created exclusively by native speakers, with biblical and linguistic experts serving only as translation consultants to provide technical support and guidance. From the lively and heartfelt translations that resulted, Bible Society scholars were able to see the power of translations that were rendered not on a word-for-word basis, but on a meaning-for-meaning basis that respected the natural rhythms and idioms of the target languages. This practice of "functional equivalence" translation reinvigorated the practice of

translating the Bible into English and is partly responsible for the explosion of new translations of the Bible that have been issued in the past thirty years. These include the Bible Society's own *Good News Translation* and *Contemporary English Version*, but also the *New International Version, New Revised Standard Version, Today's Century Version, New Living Translation,* and *The Message.*

As an organization dedicated to preparing well-researched, faithful translations, the ABS has necessarily committed itself to the pursuit of scholarly excellence. In cooperation with the United Bible Societies, the ABS has helped develop and publish authoritative Greek and Hebrew texts, handbooks on the different books of the Bible, dictionaries, and other technical aids. To make sure that all relevant disciplines are explored, the Bible Society's Nida Institute for Biblical Scholarship convenes symposia and conferences that invite both academic specialists and practicing translators to gather and exchange ideas that will assist translators in communicating the Bible's message to new audiences. For churches and readers seeking a deeper understanding of the Bible and its background, the ABS has developed study Bibles, multimedia video translations with DVD extras, Scriptures in special formats, and website resources.

For almost two centuries the American Bible Society has maintained its commitment to innovation and excellence. While the challenges it has faced over the years have changed, the Society's mission has remained constant—*to make the Bible available to every person in a language and format each can understand and afford, so all people may experience its life-changing message.*

To find out more about the American Bible Society please go to *www.AmericanBible.org* **or** *Give.AmericanBible.org*

ANGELS AND MIRACLES